Resource-Oriented Computing with NetKernel

Tom Geudens

O'REILLY®

Beijing · Cambridge · Farnham · Köln · Sebastopol · Tokyo

Resource-Oriented Computing with NetKernel

by Tom Geudens

Published by O'Reilly Media, Inc., 1005 Gravenstein Highway North, Sebastopol, CA 95472.

O'Reilly books may be purchased for educational, business, or sales promotional use. Online editions are also available for most titles (*http://my.safaribooksonline.com*). For more information, contact our corporate/institutional sales department: 800-998-9938 or *corporate@oreilly.com*.

Editor: Simon St. Laurent	**Cover Designer:** Karen Montgomery	
Production Editor: Iris Febres	**Interior Designer:** David Futato	
Copyeditor: Katie DePasquale	**Illustrator:** Robert Romano	
Proofreader: Iris Febres		

Revision History for the First Edition:

2012-05-11	First release
2012-05-29	Second release

See *http://oreilly.com/catalog/errata.csp?isbn=9781449322526* for release details.

ISBN: 978-1-449-32252-6

[LSI]

1338303048

For / Voor ...

My wife, Madelijn Lots, for showing me there is more to life than work. I love you, Madelijn.

My son, Igor. Your father is more proud of you than he will ever admit in writing. I love you, Igor.

Mijn ouders. Moeke en vake, de dagen van de "W" van "Wittekop", de basis van alles, liggen ver achter ons, maar het is één van mijn oudste herinneringen. Dat en het aantal blikjes dat we datzelfde jaar in een week voor de schoolkermis wisten te verzamelen.

Mijn zus, An Geudens. An, hier heb je nog een boek om te kaften.

Table of Contents

Part II. Batteries Included

Part III. Appendixes

Preface

Welcome. If you are reading this, you've probably heard **NetKernel** mentioned in some XML-related workshop, pretty much like I did back in 2006. Or maybe you have heard about **Resource Oriented Computing (ROC)** and want to see a practical implementation. Or maybe . . . Whatever your reasons for reading it, this book intends to take your hand to show you the wonderful world of NetKernel.[1]

Audience

This book is intended for beginning and intermediate ROC-ers.[2] There is a learning curve to ROC (and NetKernel), and this book will help you along that curve.

Downloads

Where relevant (when I feel the codelist is long), a Dropbox link will be provided in the chapter that discusses the module. Note that external softwares (usually found in the module's lib-directory) are not included in the zip. I'm just a poor microserf, I can't afford big downloads.

Conventions

This book was created with the *Scite* editor in the *DocBook* V5.1b2 format and adapted to the V4.5 format that O'Reilly uses.

Below you can see how I'll be formatting operating system output. When instructions are mixed with output, the instructions will be put in **bold**.

```
your_user@ubuntumachine:~$ aptitude -vvvv moo
Okay, okay, if I give you an Easter Egg, will you go away?
```

1. 1060, NetKernel, Resource Oriented Computing, and ROC are, respectively, a registered trademark and trademarks of 1060 Research Limited.

2. Puns with ROC(ks) are encouraged in all use of NetKernel. It does make asking for a drink with ice at a NetKernel meeting a rather tricky thing to do though.

```
your_user@ubuntumachine:~$ aptitude -vvvvv moo
All right, you win.
                           /----\
                 -------/        \
                /                 \
               /                   |
---------------/            --------\
-----------------------------------------------
your_user@ubuntumachine:~$ aptitude -vvvvvv moo
What is it? It's an elephant being eaten by a snake, of course.
```

Screenshots in this book are from a live system. They are slightly edited with Gimp for efficiency and security reasons.

When something is expected from you (imagine that), you'll find an operator (verb indicating an action) underlined in the text, followed by an operand (the thing acted upon) in italic.

- <u>Push</u> *this.*
- <u>Shake</u> *that.*

When relevant, you'll find the exact instructions to execute nearby.

In Part I, the prerequisites for a given chapter will always include prior chapters (in order). In Part II, chapters can be read as needed. Chapter 3 is the exception to the rule, as it can be read separately from the rest of Part I.

Great expectations

I want to make something clear about this book. It is not a reference guide. We all know those; they contain each and every argument (described in one line of text) to each and every function (described in one line of text) of the library/tool/programming language under discussion. Examples—if any—run along the lines of computing Fibonacci numbers. Very practical . . .[3]

Even in the second part of this book, where I'll discuss a couple of technologies in detail, I do not intend to write like that. I'm sorry. So sometimes I will point out where you can find the documentation, and you'll have to go and look for yourself.

So why write this book if the available documentation is so great? Well, the available documentation is often in reference form. And while you can find everything in there (including a couple of excellent walk-through tutorials), you might get lost or stuck or frustrated because the thing you need only has a *javadoc* (it doesn't get more *reference* than that) available.

Don't know much about history. . .

1060 Research was founded as a spin-off of original research (codenamed dexter) undertaken at Hewlett-Packard labs. The 1060 team created and implemented the Resource Oriented Computing model in what you and I know as NetKernel. In the meantime, this technology is more than 10 years old and has proven itself in sectors ranging from telecoms, to insurance, to banking, to the military.

If you wonder about the 1060. have a look at how Roman numerals work and then try this: X + M + L = . . . Makes sense, doesn't it?

10,600-foot view of ROC

If you want a more complete (and correct) explanation than you'll get here, have a look at Introduction to Resource-Oriented Computing, Part I. Be warned though that it is a tough read and that intimate knowledge of both Plato and Jack and the Beanstalk could prove helpful.

So let me give you my view on ROC after working and experimenting with it for about six years:

1. *Everything is a resource.* That includes your code, my code, the compiler, data in the database on my workstation, and data encrypted steganographically in an image from the National Art Gallery in Kuala Lumpur.

2. After you've grasped the above (and that may take some time), you'll slowly stop worrying about where and how those resources are implemented.

3. Instead, you'll focus on what you want to do with those resources, doing what you want to do with them in small, simple services that you can string together into as complex a system as you can imagine, and probably way beyond that.

---

3. This is sarcasm.

4. Last but not least, you'll stand amazed at how your system scales in exactly the same way as the Internet scales.

Why bother?

When I was in school (Anno Domini Nostri Iesu[4] 1992) for my bachelor's in IT, we got an introductory session on the NeXTSTEP platform, the platform that was going to make us obsolete within the next couple of years. And after the impressive session, most of us believed it.

Nineteen years later, I'm still in IT. People still use Cobol, PL1, and CICS as they— well, obviously not the same people . . . I hope—did before I was born. NeXTSTEP only survives in the Apple OS.

If you've been around in IT for a while, you'll have such a story of your own. There's always the next best thing that will take away all the pain of software development completely, and both teachers and managers will always love it. But if one really has to say what technology has worked in the last 15 years, one would have to say the Internet. It has grown beyond imagination.

Resource Oriented Computing combines the core ideas of the Internet, Unix, and Representational State Transfer (REST) into a new and potent whole:

- From Unix—the idea of using simple tools that share a common interoperable data model (e.g., awk, grep, sed, etc.) to build solutions
- From REST—address everything (resources, services, and code) with a URI to loosely couple the internals of your software, making it as flexible as the Web

NetKernel brings all this to an infrastructure near you!

"Don't take my word for it": in retrospect, I'd have liked to hear the guy who showed us NeXTSTEP say that. In fact, our class did meet him again as a mime at some IT gathering later that same year. It turned out that he was out of a job only weeks after giving us the presentation.

Each following chapter will contain a lot of hands-on NetKernel stuff you can try at home. In fact, I'm counting on you to try it at home!

Using Code Examples

This book is here to help you get your job done. In general, you may use the code in this book in your programs and documentation. You do not need to contact us for permission unless you're reproducing a significant portion of the code. For example, writing a program that uses several chunks of code from this book does not require

---

4. In

permission. Selling or distributing a CD-ROM of examples from O'Reilly books does require permission. Answering a question by citing this book and quoting example code does not require permission. Incorporating a significant amount of example code from this book into your product's documentation does require permission.

We appreciate, but do not require, attribution. An attribution usually includes the title, author, publisher, and ISBN. For example: "*Resource-Oriented Computing with Net-Kernel* by Tom Geudens (O'Reilly). Copyright 2012 Tom Geudens, 978-1-449-32252-6."

If you feel your use of code examples falls outside fair use or the permission given above, feel free to contact us at *permissions@oreilly.com*.

Safari® Books Online

Safari Books Online (*www.safaribooksonline.com*) is an on-demand digital library that delivers expert content in both book and video form from the world's leading authors in technology and business.

Technology professionals, software developers, web designers, and business and creative professionals use Safari Books Online as their primary resource for research, problem solving, learning, and certification training.

Safari Books Online offers a range of product mixes and pricing programs for organizations, government agencies, and individuals. Subscribers have access to thousands of books, training videos, and prepublication manuscripts in one fully searchable database from publishers like O'Reilly Media, Prentice Hall Professional, Addison-Wesley Professional, Microsoft Press, Sams, Que, Peachpit Press, Focal Press, Cisco Press, John Wiley & Sons, Syngress, Morgan Kaufmann, IBM Redbooks, Packt, Adobe Press, FT Press, Apress, Manning, New Riders, McGraw-Hill, Jones & Bartlett, Course Technology, and dozens more. For more information about Safari Books Online, please visit us online.

How to Contact Us

Please address comments and questions concerning this book to the publisher:

O'Reilly Media, Inc.
1005 Gravenstein Highway North
Sebastopol, CA 95472
800-998-9938 (in the United States or Canada)
707-829-0515 (international or local)
707-829-0104 (fax)

We have a web page for this book, where we list errata, examples, and any additional information. You can access this page at:

http://oreil.ly/ROC-NetKernel

To comment or ask technical questions about this book, send email to:

bookquestions@oreilly.com

For more information about our books, courses, conferences, and news, see our website at *http://www.oreilly.com*.

Find us on Facebook: *http://facebook.com/oreilly*

Follow us on Twitter: *http://twitter.com/oreillymedia*

Watch us on YouTube: *http://www.youtube.com/oreillymedia*

Acknowledgments

If Paul Hermans had not pointed out "a small company that is on the right track" in a technology session back in 2006, you would not be reading this today. Thank you, Paul! Nor would you be reading this if that small company—1060 Research—had not created ROC and NetKernel. Thanks there go especially to Peter Rodgers and Tony Butterfield, not only for the creating part but also for guiding a rebel system administrator with a thick skull (me)!

While the people at O'Reilly made this book happen, it was Joe Devon that linked me up with them. It probably was a small mail for him, but it was a giant leap for me. Thank you, Joe! At O'Reilly, I want to thank Simon St. Laurent for taking a new writer under his wings.

Feedback is essential for a book. I especially want to thank René Luyckx of Steria Benelux, Joe Devon (yes, him again), and Christopher Cormack of DeltaXML for doing the technical review. Thanks also to Fredrik Carnö and Andrew Hallam for going through and catching both typos and inconsistencies.

## PART I

Getting Acquainted

Let me take you by the hand and lead you through the streets of NetKernel. I'll show you something to make you change your mind . . .[5]

5. "Streets of London," Ralph McTell, 1969.

Stacking the Deck

In this chapter, we are going to prepare for some NetKernel action. I will also walk you through the creation of your first NetKernel module.

To follow along, you will need the following:

A NetKernel instance

> NetKernel has to be installed and running. Appendix A explains how to accomplish that.

A brain

> These come in all shapes and sizes. Mine—for example—is not special in any way. Brain flexibility is required though. ROC is not difficult, just different. Remember that, contrary to common belief, new brain cells can be added and new pathways through your brain can be created.[1] And after you've worked with ROC for a while, both those statements will become fact!

A text editor

> There are many good plaintext editors. If you've written any code at all, you'll probably have a favorite one. I personally use SciTE because it is lightweight, portable, and very customizable. In the documentation that comes with your Net-Kernel instance (I'll show you where you can find that documentation a bit further on), IntelliJ IDEA or Eclipse are suggested. Stick with whatever makes you productive. If your editor has code highlighting for the most common stuff (XML, HTML, CSS, Java, JavaScript, etc.), you'll be fine. However, if the default Windows Notepad is your top-of-the-line text editor I would strongly suggest that you to follow one of the above suggestions.[2]

---

1. My brain-related knowledge comes from *Pragmatic Thinking and Learning—Refactor Your Wetware* by Andy Hunt (2008, ISBN 978-1-93435-605-0). This is an excellent (very readable, even for the technically inclined) book on the matter.

2. No, I will not start a flame war over this. If you are happy with Notepad, kudos to you!

Setup

Here we take a close look at what the installation put on your system.

Layout NK5 Installation

In what follows, I'm going to use the *[install]* label for your NK5 installation location. A forward slash will be used to indicate a directory. I know this is different in Windows.[3] You'll soon notice however that within NetKernel configuration files (regardless of the operating system), the forward slash is used, and I did not want a mix. So adjust for Windows where necessary. I'm also going to label your running NetKernel as *[instance]*.

Now, when you look into your *[install]* directory, you'll see these subdirectories:

[bin]
   startup script and startup configuration files

[etc]
   [instance]-wide configuration files

[javadoc]
   generated documentation

[lib]
   instance-wide libraries

[log]
   loggings

[modules]
   the NetKernel batteries (applications and tools)

There are a couple of others. These are volatile directories for caching and for the H2 database files used by the *[instance]* itself.

[install]/bin

This contains the scripts to manually start a NetKernel instance and the configuration files with the parameters for those scripts.

[install]/etc

There's some interesting stuff here. The *kernel.properties* file contains the parameters that govern your NetKernel instance. It's very interesting stuff, but do not touch it

---

3. A functional guy in my former company put in a request to our Windows system administration team to adjust all backward slashes to forward slashes. After they recovered their composure, they forwarded the issue to Microsoft Support. No answer has come from Redmond so far.

unless you have a very good reason and know what you are doing. Besides, you can change all of these parameters from the Backend HTTPFulcrum.

The *modules.xml* file contains the modules[4] that get loaded. You will modify this file, either manually or through the Backend HTTPFulcrum; this is where you will add your own modules. In case it was not clear yet, you'll now—by looking at *modules.xml*— realize that NetKernel is built up from modules that run . . . in NetKernel.

[install]/javadoc

1. NetKernel is developed in Java.
2. Java is *one of the languages* you can use to develop modules in NetKernel.

Right, that's out of the way! I'm by no means a Java guru (I prefer Python, sorry). The NetKernel developers use Java, and the modules that make up the core of NetKernel are Java modules. The javadocs generated for these modules can be found in the javadoc directory. If you develop your own modules for NetKernel in Java, the javadocs generated for them can go in there as well. If you don't, NetKernel has a documentation system (which we'll discuss) for modules that can cater to anybody.

 People are always giving me a hard time with the "What is NetKernel?" question. They ask, "Is it an application server?" "Well, no, not really," I answer. "Oh, then it is an alternative for Java," they retort and end the discussion; which should actually just start then. For me, this just proves some people should stay as far away from IT as possible.

[install]/lib

This directory contains the libraries used to boot the NetKernel instance itself. They provide the actual ROC functionality.

[install]/log

Guess what, this directory contains the loggings of your NetKernel instance. No need to study them here; the Backend HTTPFulcrum contains a very nice logviewer.

[install]/modules

It is very hip to say something is *batteries included*. Python seems to be, and Haskell too. I guess Ruby couldn't stay behind. But what does it mean? What does it mean to say *NetKernel is batteries included*?

---

4. Module is the generic name for an application or tool within NetKernel.

Well, while having the ROC functionality at your fingertips is surely very nice, it means absolutely nothing to me! I need documentation about it, I need to be able to see it, and I need to be able to use it. Those are the batteries! And that is what the *[install]/ modules* directory contains, applications and tools that use the ROC functionality and open it up to a simple soul like me.

So, if I want to use Python to ROC in NetKernel, I can. Some Saxon for XML processing? No problem! Ant? Sure! Those and many other things are available. Some are installed by default, others can be gotten from the repositories.

[install]/project-modules

This is not in the list. Create it now. This is where you'll put your own applications. Using project-modules as directory-name is not mandatory; you can choose whatever you like, but please do not put blanks in it. However, I'll stick with project-modules for the rest of this book.

```
cd [install]
mkdir project-modules
```

Hammer Time—Your First Module

Creating a module from scratch for the first time can be an intimidating task. Still, I advise you to enter everything manually. Based on *Learn . . . The Hard Way*[5] experience it is the best way to learn.

The module we are building here is the ROC equivalent of *Hello World*. However, it would not be fair to compare it to a programming language *Hello World* or even to a Rails or NodeJS *Hello World*. In this module, you are being introduced to the ROC paradigm; the actual thing we are implementing is irrelevant.

The procedure I'm following here is that I walk you through directory by directory, file by file. There will be short explanations, and you'll be able to deduce a lot more. Do not worry if something doesn't make sense yet; that is what the next chapter is about.

---

5. A great series of books by Zed Shaw: *http://learncodethehardway.org/*

You—readers of this book—are not stupid. You no doubt noticed that I glossed over a couple of things:

1. I did not give my own answer to the "What is NetKernel?" question.
2. I did not explain what ROC functionality means.
3. I keep refering to wonderful stuff in the Backend HTTPFulcrum, but I do not show any of it.

The reason is that I want you to be able to do something (almost there) before I get to page 100 or so. As for the answer to 1, one of the purposes of this book is to make you able to formulate an answer to that yourself. So bear with me, and all will be explained.

Directory

We are going to create a directory for your module underneath [install]/project-modules. You can name this directory anything you like. I'm going to follow the URN method used in the [install]/modules directory. Note that for a directory or file, you can not use colons. We use points instead. So these could be possible directory-names for the application:

```
urn.org.elbeesee.chapter1.firstmodule-1.0.0
urn.org.tomgeudens.chapter1.firstmodule-1.0.0
```

Notice that I also added a version number in the directory name. This too is optional; it just makes it easier if I want to have two versions of the same module running side by side.

My employer would love for you all to use the first option, whereas I would of course love to become immortal by having a directory with my name in it on your hard drive. But I'll stay modest. <u>Create</u> *the directory* for your module in [install]/project-modules. I'll further refer to this directory as *[moduleroot]*.

```
cd [install]/project-modules
mkdir urn.org.netkernelbook.chapter1.firstmodule-1.0.0
```

I'm not differentiating between Windows and Linux when stating the commands. Remember to use the non-superuser *dexter*, though, to execute the commands in Linux.

Module Definition

In Chapter 2, I take it apart, but in broad terms, here is what goes on: *a module definition defines which resources the module handles.*

Let us take a look at what that means for the listing I'm going to have you enter in a minute:

- Three resource spaces are defined; *First Module—Services*, *First Module—Documentation*, and *First Module —Unit Test*. Each has a unique identifier, a URI.

- The first one is dynamically exposed to the world and covers resource requests that look like */firstmodule/helloservice/<anything here>*. These resource requests are handled with a DPML program.

- The second one plugs the modules' documentation into the NetKernel documentation system.

- The third one pulls the first into the NetKernel unit test system.

In fact, a module definition is pretty much like setting limits. From all (infinite) possible resources, you define the subsets (equal spaces) that you want to handle in your module. These subsets can cover an infinite number of possible resources as well, as is the case in our example.

Example 1-1. [moduleroot]/module.xml

```xml
<?xml version="1.0" encoding="UTF-8"?>
<module version="2.0">
  <meta>
    <identity>
      <uri>urn:org:netkernelbook:chapter1:firstmodule</uri>
      <version>1.0.0</version>
    </identity>

    <info>
      <name>First Module</name>
      <description>Netkernelbook Chapter 1 First Module</description>
    </info>
  </meta>

  <system>
    <dynamic/>
  </system>

  <rootspace
    name="First Module - Services"
    public="true"
    uri="urn:org:netkernelbook:chapter1:firstmodule:services">
    <fileset>
      <regex>res:/etc/system/SimpleDynamicImportHook.xml</regex>
    </fileset>
    <mapper>
      <config>
        <endpoint>
          <id>firstmodule:helloEP</id>
          <name>Hello Service</name>
          <description>Hello Service</description>

          <grammar>res:
            <group name="service">/firstmodule/helloservice</group>/
            <group name="value">
              <regex type="anything"/>
```

```
          </group>
        </grammar>

        <request>
          <identifier>active:dpml</identifier>
          <argument name="operator">
            res:/resources/endpoints/hello.dpml
          </argument>
          <argument method="as-string" name="value">arg:value</argument>
        </request>
      </endpoint>
    </config>

    <space>
      <fileset>
        <regex>res:/resources/endpoints/.*</regex>
      </fileset>
      <import>
        <uri>urn:org:netkernel:lang:dpml</uri>
      </import>
      <import>
        <uri>urn:org:netkernel:lang:freemarker</uri>
      </import>
    </space>
  </mapper>
</rootspace>

<rootspace
  name="First Module - Documentation"
  public="true"
  uri="urn:org:netkernelbook:chapter1:firstmodule:documentation">
  <fileset>
    <regex>res:/etc/system/(Books|Docs).xml</regex>
  </fileset>

  <fileset>
    <regex>res:/resources/documentation/.*</regex>
  </fileset>
</rootspace>

<rootspace
  name="First Module - Unit Test"
  public="true"
  uri="urn:org:netkernelbook:chapter1:firstmodule:unittest">
  <fileset>
    <regex>res:/etc/system/Tests.xml</regex>
  </fileset>
  <fileset>
    <regex>res:/resources/unittest/.*</regex>
  </fileset>

  <endpoint>
    <prototype>Limiter</prototype>
    <grammar>res:/etc/
      <regex type="anything"/>
```

```
    </grammar>
  </endpoint>

  <import>
    <uri>urn:org:netkernelbook:chapter1:firstmodule:services</uri>
  </import>

  <import>
    <uri>urn:org:netkernel:ext:layer1</uri>
    <private/>
  </import>
  </rootspace>
</module>
```

Dynamic Import

We'll discuss dynamic imports in detail later. Here we use them to make our module accessible from outside (outside NetKernel itself, that is, so we can access it in our web browser).

Create *an etc directory* for your application and *a system directory* underneath that.

```
cd [moduleroot]
mkdir etc
mkdir etc/system
```

While—in accordance with Linux—the *[moduleroot]/etc* directory will contain your module's own configuration resources, the NetKernel tools expect your module's configuration resources (metaresources, in fact) to be contained for them in *[moduleroot]/etc/system*. So that's where we'll find the *SimpleDynamicImportHook.xml* file:

Example 1-2. [moduleroot]/etc/system/SimpleDynamicImportHook.xml

```
<connection><type>HTTPFulcrum</type></connection>
```

The HelloEndpoint

This is the actual program, written in DPML, NetKernel's own scripting language. Whenever I can[6] use DPML, I will do so in this book. That way I avoid discussion over which language is best, as well as leveling the playing field.

Create *a resources directory* for your application and *a documentation, a unit test,* and *an endpoints directory* underneath that:

```
cd [moduleroot]
mkdir resources
mkdir resources/documentation
mkdir resources/endpoints
mkdir resources/unittest
```

---

6. I'll use Groovy (*http://groovy.codehaus.org/*) for the other cases.

What remains is the program itself:

Example 1-3. [moduleroot]/resources/endpoints/hello.dpml

```
<?xml version="1.0" encoding="UTF-8"?>
<sequence>
  <request assignment="response">
    <identifier>active:freemarker</identifier>
    <argument name="operator">
      <literal type="string">Input value: ${value}</literal>
    </argument>
    <argument name="value">arg:value</argument>
  </request>
  <log>
    <message>
     <literal type="string">DPML example running with input %1</literal>
    </message>
    <param>arg:value</param>
  </log>
</sequence>
```

Registering the Module

NetKernel has to be made aware of our new module. The place to do that is in *[install]/etc/modules.xml*. Add *the following entry* just before the `</modules>` end-tag (the entry has to be *on one line*; the split below is due to the limited length in this book):

```
<module runlevel="7">
  project-modules/urn.org.netkernelbook.chapter1.firstmodule-1.0.0/
</module>
```

Try It

If all went well, NetKernel should have discovered your module now. To verify this:

- Start *your favorite webbrowser.*
- Browse to *http://localhost:8080/firstmodule/helloservice/.*
- Browse to *http://localhost:8080/firstmodule/helloservice/world.* Figure 1-1 shows the result.
- Browse to *http://localhost:8080/firstmodule/helloservice/Tom%20Geudens.*

Figure 1-1. Output firstmodule/helloservice/world

We Are Not Finished

No, we are not. No application (NetKernel or otherwise) is complete without *tests* and *documentation.*[7] And NetKernel has excellent toolkits for both. In fact, you probably noticed that the necessary stuff is already there in our *[moduleroot]/module.xml* file and that we already created all necessary directories. We just need to flesh things out, starting with a couple of extra files in the *[moduleroot]/etc/system* directory.

Example 1-4. [moduleroot]/etc/system/Books.xml

```
<?xml version="1.0" encoding="UTF-8"?>
<books>
  <book>
    <id>book:urn:org:netkernelbook:chapter1:firstmodule</id>
    <title>First Module</title>
    <desc>netkernelbook chapter1 first module documentation</desc>
    <toc>
      <item id="urn:org:netkernelbook:chapter1:firstmodule:guide"/>
      <item id="urn:org:netkernelbook:chapter1:firstmodule:endpoints"/>
    </toc>
  </book>
</books>
```

Example 1-5. [moduleroot]/etc/system/Docs.xml

```
<?xml version="1.0" encoding="UTF-8"?>
<docs>
  <doc>
    <id>urn:org:netkernelbook:chapter1:firstmodule:guide</id>
    <title>Guide to First Module</title>
    <desc>first module explained</desc>
    <uri>res:/resources/documentation/doc_guide.txt</uri>
  </doc>
```

---

7. You will notice throughout this book that I have very definite ideas about application development. Don't take offense, whatever approach works for you is fine by me—in your own book that is.

```
<doc>
  <id>urn:org:netkernelbook:chapter1:firstmodule:endpoints</id>
  <title>Reference for First Module Endpoints</title>
  <desc>first module use</desc>
  <uri>res:/resources/documentation/doc_endpoints.txt</uri>
</doc>
</docs>
```

Example 1-6. [moduleroot]/etc/system/Tests.xml

```
<?xml version="1.0" encoding="UTF-8"?>
<tests>
  <test>
    <id>test:urn:org:netkernelbook:chapter1:firstmodule</id>
    <name>First Module</name>
    <desc>netkernelbook chapter1 first module unittest</desc>
    <uri>res:/resources/unittest/testlist.xml</uri>
  </test>
</tests>
```

The actual documentation files go into the *resources/documentation* directory.

Example 1-7. [moduleroot]/resources/documentation/doc_guide.txt

```
== Documentation Stub ==
This is a documentation stub.

For more information on editing documentation
see the [doc:sysadmin:guide:doc:editing|Editing Guide].
```

Example 1-8. [moduleroot]/resources/documentation/doc_endpoints.txt

```
{endpoint}firstmodule:helloEP{/endpoint}
==Detail==
This hello endpoint simply formats the value argument
it receives and returns it as a string response.

==Resource Identifier Syntax==
The endpoint accepts requests which match the identifier syntax
of '''res:/firstmodule/helloservice/ANY_OTHER_TEXT'''

The '''ANY_OTHER_TEXT''' is captured as the value argument
passed into the endpoint.
```

And the actual test files go into the *resources/unittest* directory.

Example 1-9. [moduleroot]/resources/unittest/testlist.xml

```
<?xml version="1.0" encoding="UTF-8"?>
<testlist>
  <test name="Invoke service by identifier">
    <request>
      <identifier>res:/firstmodule/helloservice/World</identifier>
    </request>
    <assert>
      <stringEquals>Input value: World</stringEquals>
```

```
    </assert>
  </test>

  <test name="Invoke service by endpoint">
    <request>
      <identifier>meta:firstmodule:helloEP</identifier>
      <argument name="value">World</argument>
    </request>
    <assert>
      <stringEquals>Input value: World</stringEquals>
    </assert>
  </test>
</testlist>
```

Trying Documentation and Tests

Now we are finished. And you can check that yourself:

- Start *your favorite webbrowser*.
- Browse to *http://localhost:1060/book/view/book:urn:org:netkernelbook:chapter1: firstmodule/*.
- Browse to *http://localhost:1060/test/view/html/test:urn:org:netkernelbook:chap ter1:firstmodule*.

Don't be shy: do try out the tests and through the documentation!

Source Version Control

It does seem ridiculous to bring this up here, but this is a good point to set up source version control. Every module you write—even one as small as this one—should have it. If you are not familiar with it, Appendix E will guide you. If you are, use it.

Well Done

You are probably not very impressed yet with the results. Rome was not built in one chapter either, and trust me, we've covered a lot of ground already.

Conclusion

Chapter 1 was aimed at you getting your *First Module* up and running as quickly as possible. In Chapter 2, we will take the scalpel to the same module and explain it in both ROC terms and technical terms.

The download for this chapter can be found here (*http://dl.dropbox.com/u/65770556/ urn.org.netkernelbook.chapter1.firstmodule-1.0.0.zip*).

Incision, Right Here

This chapter will explain the what, how and why of *First Module*. We will also create a module using the *Webserver Pattern*.

Inside [moduleroot]/module.xml

If were awake during the previous chapter, you noticed that the *[moduleroot]/module.xml* file contains most of the meat. It does in fact have two main purposes:

1. Define your module.
2. Define the ROC layout of your module.

Number one is obvious, and number two is important. If your ROC layout is done well, putting the rest of your module together will be easy (and short). So let's study it in detail.

Template

Let's start with a simple *module.xml* template.

```
<module version="2.0">
  <meta>
    <identity>
      <uri>urn:org:yourcompany:yourapplication:newmodule</uri>
      <version>0.0.1</version>
    </identity>
    <info>
      <name>New Module</name>
      <description>New Module Template</description>
    </info>
  </meta>

  <system>
    <dynamic/>
  </system>
```

```
  <rootspace>
  </rootspace>
</module>
```

 Having good templates available can seriously reduce your development time. You do not need a fancy system to manage them, though some editors have one, and if you feel comfortable with it, by all means use it. A simple directory will do. Make sure to put them under version control as well though!

The template contains nothing special:

`<meta>`

This contains the description of your module. Do note the use of colons in the *URI*.

`<dynamic>`

With `<system><dynamic/></system>` we indicate two things:

1. Any change to *[moduleroot]/module.xml* will cause a *hot* reload of the module.
2. Any Java classfiles (within the application) that change during the run of the NetKernel instance will be reloaded dynamically.

If you do not want hot reloads, leave out the system tag altogether. Do note that changes to scripts inside your module are always immediate, as these are not not compiled and/or preloaded into the jvm.

`<rootspace>`

Empty right now, this is where most of the action will take place. You can have multiple rootspaces in one *module.xml*. If you do, each will require its own unique URI. Any other modules that use (part of) your module, will have to import (we'll see that in a minute) the URI(s) of the relevant rootspace(s) rather than the URI of the module. If you do not provide URIs for the rootspaces, the first rootspace will get the URI of the module, every rootspace after that (if any) will get the URI of the module plus a sequence number.[1]

Template's First Flesh

We fill out the description of our module and provide three rootspaces.

```
<?xml version="1.0" encoding="UTF-8"?>
<module version="2.0">
  <meta>
    <identity>
      <uri>urn:org:netkernelbook:chapter1:firstmodule</uri>
      <version>1.0.0</version>
    </identity>
```

---

1. Providing URIs for your rootspaces is good practice!

```
   <info>
     <name>First Module</name>
     <description>netkernelbook chapter 1 first module</description>
   </info>
  </meta>

  <system>
    <dynamic/>
  </system>

  <rootspace uri="urn:org:netkernelbook:chapter1:firstmodule:services">
  </rootspace>

  <rootspace uri="urn:org:netkernelbook:chapter1:firstmodule:documentation">
  </rootspace>

  <rootspace uri="urn:org:netkernelbook:chapter1:firstmodule:unittest">
  </rootspace>
</module>
```

Rootspace

A *rootspace* defines a *resource space*. You could compare this (if any comparisons have to be made at all) to a *scope* or a *context*. Within this resource space, you define one (otherwise there's no need for a rootspace) or more *endpoints*. An endpoint is a space element that provides a gateway between logical resources and physical code. And that is it, there is no more. And no, there is *no catch*.

 Let this information slowly sink into your mind. If it doesn't make sense yet, follow along through the chapter, then come back and read the above again. If (or better yet, when) you can fully grasp the repercussions of the above description of a rootspace, you've mastered the nature of ROC.

NetKernel is very flexible and can be adapted to suit your needs. This flexibility does have a downside for inexperienced users. There is, for example, no single correct way to define your resource endpoints. It depends on what you need. Let's have a look at our *[moduleroot]/module.xml* and see what we can find.

Endpoint—Fileset

You can easily find several of those. Look for the `<fileset>` tag. Here's the first one:

```
<fileset>
  <regex>res:/etc/system/SimpleDynamicImportHook.xml</regex>
</fileset>
```

The definition of a fileset states that it exposes physical resources contained within a module's physical directory to the logical space. All exposed files will be resolved using the generic *res:/* URI scheme.

So what happens is pretty obvious: this fileset exposes a single resource, *[moduleroot]/etc/system/SimpleDynamicImportHook.xml*[2]. The question is, of course, exposes it to whom? Well, to whomever has access to the space containing the endpoint, or a public rootspace in this case. And this brings us seamlessly to the next type of endpoint.

Endpoint—Import

After the fileset this is the most common endpoint. Look for the `<import>` tag. Here's one from the unit test rootspace.

```
<import>
  <uri>urn:org:netkernelbook:chapter1:firstmodule:services</uri>
</import>
```

With an import, you grant a space access to the endpoints of the imported space. There is no theoretical limit on how deep this can go. The next type of endpoint shows that clearly.

Endpoint—Mapper

Easy to find with the `<mapper>` tag, the mapper endpoint is very powerful, and you'll use it in almost every module, so a template will come in handy.

```
<mapper>
  <config>
    <endpoint>
      <grammar />
      <request />
    </endpoint>
  </config>
  <space />
</mapper>
```

We'll start at the bottom of the mapper template, the `<space>` tag.

```
<space>
  <fileset>
    <regex>res:/resources/endpoints/.*</regex>
  </fileset>
  <import>
    <uri>urn:org:netkernel:lang:dpml</uri>
  </import>
  <import>
    <uri>urn:org:netkernel:lang:freemarker</uri>
```

---

2. Dynamic imports are discussed a bit further along. You'll get there soon enough. First we learn to walk, then we learn to run.

```
    </import>
  </space>
```

This is where you provide access to resources. Which resources? Well, both `<file set>` and `<import>` endpoints are known to you. So you can deduce that we'll have access to the files in the *[moduleroot]/resources/endpoints* directory as well as to whatever endpoints the *dpml* and *freemarker* modules expose. So there's nothing new here; it's only the mapper that has access to the so-called *wrapped space*, but otherwise it's exactly the same.

Next, we take a look at the `<config>` tag:

```
<config>
  <endpoint>
    <id>urn:org:netkernelbook:chapter1:firstmodule:services:helloEP</id>
    <name>Hello Service</name>
    <description>Hello Service</description>

    <grammar>res:
      <group name="service">/firstmodule/helloservice</group>/
      <group name="value">
        <regex type="anything"/>
      </group>
    </grammar>

    <request>
      <identifier>active:dpml</identifier>
      <argument name="operator">
        res:/resources/endpoints/hello.dpml
      </argument>
      <argument method="as-string" name="value">arg:value</argument>
    </request>
  </endpoint>
</config>
```

This looks complicated, but the `config` tag contains the endpoints—we only have one, but you can have more—and the endpoint only contains two elements.

- Through the `<grammar>`, the mapper is going to expose the fact that our application can handle requests that look like *res:/firstmodule/helloservice/*.
- The `<request>` does the actual handling. The program that does the work is *hello.dpml*, which we find in a directory provided in the wrapped space. DPML is a scripting language provided in the wrapped space.[3]

Everything is a resource, and all (!) NetKernel does is handle resource requests. In *First Module*, these don't go very deep, but I hope you still get a *feel* for how deep this can go (as deep as you can imagine and beyond).

---

3. If you paid attention so far, you might wonder where the Freemarker stuff comes in. Well, it is used inside the hello.dpml program.

Endpoint—Prototype

There is one more endpoint type used in *First Module* that we have to cover.

Think of a prototype as an endpoint definition with the complexity taken away. Typically libraries will provide them. All you have to do is provide the required (and/or optional) parameters, and the prototype will make sure the correct endpoint is instantiated.

The *Limiter* prototype (the one being used in `<rootspace name="First Module - Unit Test">`) actually limits what your module exports from the stuff it imports. The implementation can be found in the *layer1* module, hence the import.

 Layer1 is the basic utility provider. While not strictly necessary in every single one of your modules, you'll find the going tough if you want to do completely without it. It also provides the Java-language runtime.

This is as good a point as any to introduce Appendix F. This final appendix of the book (I'm in IT, my symbols run out at *F*) is going to be living and breathing and always in progress. It will contain lifesaving examples that do not fit elsewhere in the book. And you know what? It starts with a *Limiter* example!

Dynamic Imports

The concept of importing spaces is probably clear by now. You *pull* other spaces inside your module and can use the stuff they expose. Simple. A dynamic import works the other way around. A module *publishes* or *pushes* the fact that it wants to be imported.

The most common case is where you want some of your module's endpoints exposed not only to the rest of NetKernel but to the Internet. The module that can take care of that is the *Frontend HTTPFulcrum*.

What you could do is add an import of your module in the *[moduleroot]/module.xml* of the Frontend HTTPFulcrum. In fact, that's how it was done in NetKernel 3. Since NetKernel 4, our module just exposes the *res:/etc/system/SimpleDynamicImport-Hook.xml* resource. The Frontend HTTPFulcrum will check if it contains the correct information, and if it does, your module is imported and your endpoints are exposed to the Internet.

The Web Server Pattern

NetKernel can do anything you imagine, but most of the time you're not the first person to think of a particular use.[4] A very common pattern is that of the web server.

Goal

We want to turn a library of files into servable resources. For the example module, I will use the ExtJS (*http://www.sencha.com/products/extjs/*) library.

State your goals up front, always! In all the time I've worked with Net-Kernel, I've never been able to state an impossible goal. Some of them required asking others and redefining some of what I thought I knew of NetKernel, but impossible? No. So don't let your goals be limited by what you (think you) know!

There is an extra requirement. Since I do not like to break what is working, I have at any given time multiple versions of ExtJS in action. Requests will look like this:

```
res:/ExtJS-3.0.0/ext-all.js
res:/ExtJS-3.1.0/adapter/ext/ext-base.js
res:/ExtJS-3.3.1/plugins/uxmedia.js
```

If you want to be able to follow this example all the way, you can find the relevant downloads for ExtJS 3.0.0 (*http://extjs.cachefly.net/ext-3.0.0.zip*), ExtJS 3.1.0 (*http://extjs.cachefly.net/ext-3.1.0.zip*) and ExtJS 3.3.1 (*http://extjs.cachefly.net/ext-3.3.1.zip*) on the Sencha site. They tend to get moved around quite a bit, so forgive me if the provided links do not work for you.

Since Sencha took over the ExtJS framework the license is getting more and more restrictive with each new version. And while doing the examples below is completely fine, you'd better check the license if you are going to use ExtJS for anything else.

Module Definition

You should know by now how to set up a new module.

```
cd [install]/project-modules
mkdir urn.org.netkernelbook.chapter2.extjs_server-1.0.0
```

Example 2-1. [moduleroot]/module.xml

```xml
<?xml version="1.0" encoding="UTF-8"?>
<module version="2.0">
  <meta>
    <identity>
      <uri>urn:org:netkernelbook:chapter2:extjs_server</uri>
      <version>1.0.0</version>
    </identity>
    <info>
      <name>ExtJS Server</name>
```

---

4. My apologies for hurting your ego.

```xml
    <description>netkernelbook chapter 2 extjs server</description>
  </info>
</meta>

<system>
  <dynamic/>
</system>

<rootspace
  name="ExtJS Server"
  public="true"
  uri="urn:org:netkernelbook:chapter2:extjs_server">
  <fileset>
    <regex>res:/etc/system/SimpleDynamicImportHook.xml</regex>
  </fileset>

  <fileset>
    <regex>res:/ExtJS-[0-9]\.[0-9]\.[0-9]/.*</regex>
  </fileset>
</rootspace>

<rootspace
  name="ExtJS Server - Documentation"
  public="true"
  uri="urn:org:netkernelbook:chapter2:extjs_server:documentation">
  <fileset>
    <regex>res:/etc/system/(Books|Docs).xml</regex>
  </fileset>

  <fileset>
    <regex>res:/resources/documentation/.*</regex>
  </fileset>
</rootspace>

<rootspace
  name="ExtJS Server - Unit Test"
  public="true"
  uri="urn:org:netkernelbook:chapter2:extjs_server:unittest">
  <fileset>
    <regex>res:/etc/system/Tests.xml</regex>
  </fileset>

  <fileset>
    <regex>res:/resources/unittest/.*</regex>
  </fileset>

  <endpoint>
    <prototype>Limiter</prototype>
    <grammar>res:/etc/
      <regex type="anything"/>
    </grammar>
  </endpoint>

  <import>
    <uri>urn:org:netkernelbook:chapter2:extjs_server</uri>
```

```
    </import>

    <import>
      <uri>urn:org:netkernel:xml:core</uri>
    </import>
    <import>
      <uri>urn:org:netkernel:ext:layer1</uri>
      <private/>
    </import>
  </rootspace>
</module>
```

As you can see, the *module.xml* file is even simpler than the one for *First Module*. We make the ExtJS files in our module available and also open them up (dynamically) to the Frontend HTTPFulcrum.

In order to make the ExtJS files available, unzip the archives in *[moduleroot]*. I renamed the default directory names that the archives provide so that my application directory looks like this (note that I do not reproduce the contents of the ExtJS-X.X.X directories as that would make the list too long:

```
etc
  system
    Books.xml, Docs.xml, SimpleDynamicImportHook.xml, Tests.xml
ExtJS-3.0.0
ExtJS-3.1.0
ExtJS-3.3.1
resources
  documentation
    doc_guide.txt
  unittest
    testlist.xml
module.xml
```

Did you already register the new module? Good for you! If not, now's the time to do it. In *[install]/etc/modules.xml* as you'll no doubt remember, <u>add</u> *the following entry* just before the </modules> endtag (entry has to be *on one line*; the split below is due to the limited line length in this book).

```
<module runlevel="7">
  project-modules/urn.org.netkernelbook.chapter2.extjs_server-1.0.0/
</module>
```

To check whether our module works, try the following URLs:

- *http://localhost:8080/ExtJS-3.0.0/license.txt*
- *http://localhost:8080/ExtJS-3.0.0/docs/index.html*
- *http://localhost:8080/ExtJS-3.1.0/license.txt*
- *http://localhost:8080/ExtJS-3.1.0/docs/index.html*
- *http://localhost:8080/ExtJS-3.3.1/license.txt*
- *http://localhost:8080/ExtJS-3.3.1/docs/index.html*

Right, those *index.html* links actually run an ExtJS application (a rather nice one in fact; the ExtJS documentation system is not bad at all). If you want to make absolutely 100% sure that it is running from your NetKernel server, turn off your Internet connection There are other ways to verify that the requests for the files do indeed get handled by NetKernel, but we'll see those later on in this book.

The application works, but I skipped over what goes in the documentation and test files. The reason is that I want to take a closer look at both and to introduce the Backend HTTPFulcrum while we're at it.

Documentation

Did I say the ExtJS documentation system is not bad? It's nothing compared to the NetKernel documentation system though, which is, of course, a module (actually a couple of modules) built in NetKernel itself.

You may have guessed (from the documentation files we created for *First Module*) that the documentation application works with dynamic imports. In fact, it looks for these two files, which your application has to expose:

- *[moduleroot]/etc/system/Books.xml*
- *[moduleroot]/etc/system/Docs.xml*

You do not have to be a *ROC*ket scientist to figure out what these files refer to. Each application can have a book (several in fact) containing as many documents (pages) as you want.

Example 2-2. [moduleroot]/etc/system/Books.xml

```
<?xml version="1.0" encoding="UTF-8"?>
<books>
  <book>
    <id>book:urn:org:netkernelbook:chapter2:extjs_server</id>
    <title>ExtJS Server</title>
    <desc>netkernelbook chapter2 extjs server documentation</desc>
    <toc>
      <item id="urn:org:netkernelbook:chapter2:extjs_server:guide"/>
    </toc>
  </book>
</books>
```

Example 2-3. [moduleroot]/etc/system/Docs.xml

```
<?xml version="1.0" encoding="UTF-8"?>
<docs>
  <doc>
    <id>urn:org:netkernelbook:chapter2:extjs_server:guide</id>
    <title>Guide to ExtJS Server</title>
    <desc>extjs server explained</desc>
    <uri>res:/resources/documentation/doc_guide.txt</uri>
```

```
    </doc>
  </docs>
```

Again, it's not very hard to figure out how this works. We are going to have one book containing one document (there were two documents in *First Module*). The contents of this document can be found in a text file in our application's *resources/doc* directory.

Example 2-4. [moduleroot]/resources/documentation/doc_guide.txt

```
== ExtJS Server ==

=== ExtJS 3.0.0 ===
Main file to include is res:/ExtJS-3.0.0/ext-all.js

=== ExtJS 3.1.0 ===
Main file to include is res:/ExtJS-3.1.0/ext-all.js

=== ExtJS 3.3.1 ===
Main file to include is res:/ExtJS-3.3.1/ext-all.js


For more information on editing documentation
see the [doc:sysadmin:guide:doc:editing|Editing Guide].
```

The syntax looks a little weird, but actually it's MediaWiki-syntax. Three other syntax-parser engines are available (Textile, Confluence, TracWiki), and you can add your own. Code highlighting is available through the use of a macro-engine. Five macro-engines are available (Java, XML, Literal, Bitmap, SVG), and again you can add your own.

So if you wanted, say, the *Docs.xml* file inside your documentation with the XML properly highlighted, you would put the following inside your document file:

```
{xml}
<docs>
  <doc>
    <id>urn:org:netkernelbook:chapter2:extjs_server:guide</id>
    <title>Guide to ExtJS Server</title>
    <desc>extjs server explained</desc>
    <uri>res:/resources/documentation/doc_guide.txt</uri>
  </doc>
</docs>
{/xml}
```

You now want to see what the documentation actually looks like, of course: *http://localhost:1060/book/view/book:urn:org:netkernelbook:chapter2:extjs_server/*

Did you notice the *:1060* in the URL? The documentation application is not exposed on the Frontend HTTPFulcrum (port 8080) but on the Backend HTTPFulcrum (port 1060), which you've only used during the installation so far. All *administration* applications are exposed on that fulcrum, the idea being that those applications are for *private* use while the applications on the Frontend HTTPFulcrum are for *public* use. However, there's nothing to keep you from exposing your applications on the Backend

HTTPFulcrum. All you have to do is change the content of your application's *[moduleroot]/etc/system/SimpleDynamicImportHook.xml*.

```
<connection>
  <type>HTTPAdminFulcrum</type>
</connection>
```

In fact, you can expose your application on both fulcrums:

```
<connection>
  <type>HTTPAdminFulcrum</type>
  <type>HTTPFulcrum</type>
</connection>
```

Testing

The setup of the XUnit Tests application is very like that of the Documentation application. It looks for this file, which our application has to expose:

Example 2-5. [moduleroot]/etc/system/Tests.xml

```
<?xml version="1.0" encoding="UTF-8"?>
<tests>
  <test>
    <id>test:urn:org:netkernelbook:chapter2:extjs_server</id>
    <name>ExtJS Server</name>
    <desc>netkernelbook chapter2 extjs server unittest</desc>
    <uri>res:/resources/unittest/testlist.xml</uri>
  </test>
</tests>
```

This gets your application into the XUnit Tests application. It also tells us that the tests are described in the *[moduleroot]/resources/unittest directory*.

Example 2-6. [moduleroot]/resources/unittest/testlist.xml

```
<?xml version="1.0" encoding="UTF-8"?>
<testlist>
  <test name="Invoke ExtJS-3.0.0">
    <request>
      <identifier>res:/ExtJS-3.0.0/docs/index.html</identifier>
    </request>
    <assertDefinition name="validExtJS300">
      <identifier>active:xpatheval</identifier>
      <argument name="operand" >arg:test:result</argument>
      <argument name="operator">
        res:/resources/unittest/xpath/validExtJS300.xpath
      </argument>
    </assertDefinition>
    <assert>
      <validExtJS300/>
    </assert>
  </test>

  <test name="Invoke ExtJS-3.1.0">
```

```
    <request>
      <identifier>res:/ExtJS-3.1.0/docs/index.html</identifier>
    </request>
    <assertDefinition name="validExtJS310">
      <identifier>active:xpatheval</identifier>
      <argument name="operand" >arg:test:result</argument>
      <argument name="operator">
        res:/resources/unittest/xpath/validExtJS310.xpath
      </argument>
    </assertDefinition>
    <assert>
      <validExtJS310/>
    </assert>
  </test>

  <test name="Invoke ExtJS-3.3.1">
    <request>
      <identifier>res:/ExtJS-3.3.1/docs/index.html</identifier>
    </request>
    <assertDefinition name="validExtJS331">
      <identifier>active:xpatheval</identifier>
      <argument name="operand" tolerant="true">arg:test:result</argument>
      <argument name="operator">
        res:/resources/unittest/xpath/validExtJS331.xpath
      </argument>
    </assertDefinition>
    <assert>
      <validExtJS331/>
    </assert>
  </test>

</testlist>
```

As you can see, this is slightly (but only slightly) more complicated than the same resource in the *First Module* application. There we were able to use built-in asserts, here we define our own asserts, which differ for each version of ExtJS we have in our application.

What happens in each test is this:

1. The request is executed (the version specific *index.html*).
2. The assert is checked (true means test succeeded, and false means test failed).
3. Since the assert is not a built-in assert (validExtJSxxx is custom defined), the relevant assertDefinition is executed. This is an xpath evaluation of the result of the request with an xpath path specific for each version of ExtJS.

I stated earlier that *everything is a resource and all (!) NetKernel does is handle resource requests*. While that holds true, it does not mean that you do not need *technical* knowledge. When manipulating XML, you need knowledge of XPath, XQuery, XSLT, and so on, and NetKernel will help you leverage your technical knowledge in new ways, but it does not make this knowledge obsolete or unnecessary!

Example 2-7. [moduleroot]/resources/unittest/xpath/validExtJS300.xpath

```
/html/head/title/text() = 'Ext 3.0 - API Documentation'
```

Example 2-8. [moduleroot]/resources/unittest/xpath/validExtJS310.xpath

```
/html/head/title/text() = 'Ext 3.1 - API Documentation'
```

Example 2-9. [moduleroot]/resources/unittest/xpath/validExtJS331.xpath

```
/html/head/title/text() = 'Ext JS 3.3.1 API Documentation'
```

Now, I could go into every nitty gritty detail of how all this is accomplished (this chapter would never end), or I can point you to the relevant documents:

- *http://localhost:1060/book/view/book:mod:test:book/*
- *http://localhost:1060/book/view/book:mod:xml:core:book/doc:mod:xml:core:xpa theval*

The actual tests for the ExtJS Server application can be found at *http://localhost:1060/test/view/html/test:urn:org:netkernelbook:chapter2:extjs_server*,[5] or you can navigate yourself through the Control Panel at *http://localhost:1060*, the Developer tab, and the XUnit Test option.

Conclusion

In this chapter, we cut out the heart and soul of *First Module*, and it did have some surprises in store for us. We talked about *(root)spaces*, *endpoints*, *requests*, and *grammars* (not necessarily in that order). We finished by exploring a simple pattern on NetKernel, the web serving pattern.

 This might be a good place to mention that the web serving pattern is indeed that. This means that if your host is accessible on the Internet, everybody can now use your host to get the ExtJS framework. This might be a bit of overkill (and open you up to a Denial Of Service attack) if you only want to use the framework in other NetKernel applications running on the same host.

---

5. If you are attentive when executing the tests, you can find the answer to your question in Appendix F.

If you came out of this chapter with your head still on, you're now ready to do some experimenting of your own. By all means do, and have some fun while you're at it! The next chapter will be there, waiting for you when you come back.

The download for this chapter can be found here (*http://dl.dropbox.com/u/65770556/ urn.org.netkernelbook.chapter2.extjs_server-1.0.0.zip*).

## CHAPTER 3

ROC Talk

Principles

Although the intention of this book is to be practical, it is impossible to go completely without theory. This chapter covers that need. Let us start the ROC excavation with some principles:

1. A resource is an abstract set of information.

- *Resource-Oriented Computing with NetKernel* is a book.
- *Mona Lisa* is a painting.

2. Each resource may be identified by one or more logical identifier.

- The book *Resource-Oriented Computing with NetKernel* is the book referred to here (*http://www.netkernel.org/nk4um/topic/741/*).
- The book *Resource-Oriented Computing with NetKernel* is the book described here (*http://wiki.netkernel.org/wink/wiki/NetKernel/News/1/45/*).
- The painting *Mona Lisa* is the most famous painting by Leonardo da Vinci.
- The painting *Mona Lisa* is also known as La Gioconda.

3. A logical identifier may be resolved within an informational context to obtain a physical resource-representation.

- *Resource-Oriented Computing with NetKernel* can be resolved as the DocBook file I am editing right now (*file:///C:/DOCBOOK/practical_netkernel.xml*).
- *Resource-Oriented Computing with NetKernel* can be resolved as the PDF file you can read (*http://netkernelbook.org/serving/pdf/practical_netkernel_nk5.pdf*).

4. Computation is the reification of a resource to a physical resource-representation.

 According to my dictionary, reification means *bringing into being* or *turning concrete*.

- Opening this DOCBOOK file (*file:///C:/DOCBOOK/practical_netkernel.xml*) in a text editor
- Requesting this PDF file (*http://netkernelbook.org/serving/pdf/practical_netkernel _nk5.pdf*) in a web browser

The verbs (opening, requesting) are the *computation*, the hyperlinks are *logical identifiers*, and what you get on screen (even if you get an error, as you probably will in the case of the file since that is locally on my machine) is the *physical resource-representation*.

5. Resource-representations are immutable.

This is a tough but important nut to crack, so let's have some examples:

- I'd be very (unpleasantly) surprised if I opened the above file and found an explanation of how to grow peas. So would you, if you requested the above URL to the PDF.
- As I update this book, you will from time to time get a newer version (i.e., another resource-representation) of the book when you request the same URL.

This sounds illogical, but it is important, so let us go over that again. Take a site with news articles. On a given moment, entering the URL (a logical identifier) in your browser will get you a *representation* that is valid at that moment. It is immutable. If you were to change it yourself, it would no longer be a representation of the news site. It remains valid as long as no new articles get written. The moment a new article gets written, the *resource changes*, and a new request for the resource will result in a *different representation*.

It follows that the expected lifetime (validity) of a representation can vary wildly depending on the resource. NetKernel has an excellent caching system that covers most (if not all) cases.

6. Transreption is the isomorphic, lossless transformation of one physical resource-representation to another.

The same DocBook document representing this book can be *transrepted* to a PDF, Mobi, EPub, Excel, and so on, document.

The key word here is *lossless*. ROC does actually not care what form its resources take. You like XML? Fine. You like JSON? Fine. You like a binary stream? Fine. Whenever a certain format is needed, a transreption will be done.

7. Computational results are resources and are identified within the address space.

Pretty soon after this book is finished, somebody will update *the Ultimate Collection of IT books* torrent (on The Pirate Bay), which will from then on contain the *Resource-Oriented Computing with NetKernel* book.[1]

Three Cs

Application and system development on a resource-oriented computing platform can be broadly categorized in three stages: *Construct*, *Compose*, and *Constrain*.[2]

Construct

The construct stage is focused on building physical level components implemented with the NetKernel Foundation (NKF) API. Construct includes adding new services, tools, and resource models.

To put this in Unix/Linux terms, this is the stage where you would design and write the sed, sort, and grep utilities.

See http://localhost:1060/book/view/book:glossary/doc:glossary:nkf for more information on the NKF API. In the code, you'll have access to it through the *context* object.

Typically, *less than 20%* of development time is dedicated to this form of work. Now, read that percentage again . . .

---

1. If you think I'm being funny here, think again.

2. You could say you are ROCing *in* instead of *on* stages.

Compose

The composition stage is focused on coordinating resource requests. In this stage, one uses logical level tools and services to transform and compose resources from other resources.

Composition can be orchestrated with DPML or by using any other supported language to make requests with the NKF API. A pretty recent development in this, which warrants a complete chapter of its own in this book, is the *nCoDE* tool.

 To put this in Unix/Linux terms, this is the stage where you would write a shell script and route your input through the utilities to deliver the required output.

Typically *about 70%*, of development time is associated with composition.

Constrain

Unlike with strongly typed, statically linked software, in ROC the constraint stage is often the final stage of development.

Once a system is working, one can apply business and information constraints to provide contractual and semantic boundaries within your application architecture. Think *security*, think *audit*, think *data validation*, but also think *loadbalancing* and *failover*.

 To put this in Unix/Linux terms, this is the stage where you would think about how the script is going to be executed (and by whom). Will sudo-entries be required? Does the script have to be "niced" or not? Where (on what host or hosts) is it going to run?

Typically, *about 10%* of development time is associated with applying constraints. It's another percentage you may want to read again.

Shock

I don't know about you, but these percentages came as a bit of a shock to me. The reason? Because they mean that the percentage of time spent coding on a typical IT project is going to come down, and will keep coming down as your ROC toolkit grows (just like you do not have to write a sed, sort, or grep utility on Unix/Linux because they are already there).

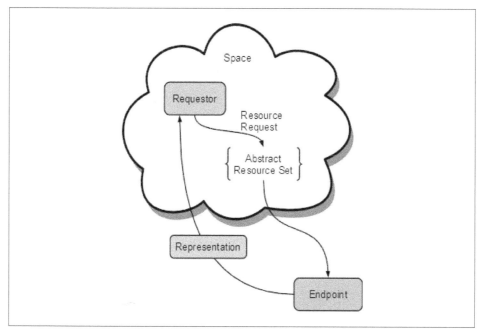

Figure 3-1. Frequently used graph

 From my own experience, I can say the percentages mentioned above are true, although not for a ROC beginner. There is a learning curve, and experienced developers will have to *unlearn* the tendency to throw code at any problem.

I place the main activity, composing, somewhere in between current developers' tasks and current architects' tasks. Depending on the available tools, this may shift to one or the other (to stay with my comparison example, writing a shell script on Unix/Linux is today definitely a developer task), but very likely there is going to be a middle ground where both speak the same resource language. Nice.

Frequently Used Graph

Remember those annual (if you are lucky) company information meetings where the CEO whips out the very same graph every single year? The axes on the graph may change, occasionally you get a mirror graph, or things might be given another meaning, but it is the same graph, no doubt about it! Well, ROC has a frequently used graph (Figure 3-1), too. And for this one, nothing ever changes.

I am not going to explain it. It should—at this stage—make sense without explanation.

Besides, there is little to add to it, except maybe depth. When you look at it, you see one space, one requestor, one endpoint, one representation. Add *many* before requestor, endpoint, and representation, and you've got the *World Wide Web*.

Add *many* before space, too, and you've got the complete potential of ROC, yet still the same rules apply as for *one*.

ROC Training

Let us have a look at the requirements to start **ROC'ing with NetKernel**.

Base

1. IT fundamentals.
2. Programming fundamentals.
3. XML fundamentals.
4. Dynamic scripting language. Pick one that is supported in NetKernel. If you don't have a preference, Groovy is a good choice.
5. XSLT.
6. ROC Fundamentals.
7. XRL.
8. DPML. This is an optional point. I still advise it.

Note that only 6, 7, and 8 are NetKernel specific.

Put together that there would be a three-year curriculum for a secondary school, a two-year curriculum for a bachelor's, a three- to six-month (depending on prior knowledge) curriculum for a *fresh* IT professional.

Afterward, you'll be able to *think ROC* and work independently on backend solutions.

Adding the Front End

1. HTML.
2. CSS.
3. JavaScript. This is also a good time to choose and learn a JavaScript framework (JQuery, qooxdoo, ExtJS, and others). Serving it from within NetKernel is a very good ROC exercise.

Add six months for the secondary school, three months for the bachelor's and IT professionals.

Afterward, you'll be able to work independently on end-to-end solutions.

Advanced

1. ROC Advanced.
2. Java. NetKernel runs in a JVM, and even though it is true that you can do the job with a dynamic scripting language, for creating core tools or for modifying the existing tools, you need Java.

The timeline for this can vary wildly.

Afterward, you'll be able to create core tools and integrate new technologies into the ROC abstraction.

Extra

1. Databases
2. Queing systems
3. Other possibilities

Know at least the basics of the technologies you are using, even (or maybe especially) when you can use them as black boxes.

Practice

As the punchline goes about the man asking how to get to Carnegie Hall, "Practice my man, practice."

The above may look like an enormous task, but while I was writing it, I noticed the similarity with my own training to become a mainframe developer (20 years ago now). It took three months to become a productive batch programmer, another three to become independent (and write CICS frontends), and only with lots of practice did I become proficient.

Real Life ROC

Let me start with a quote from the preface: From Linux ROC borrows the idea of using simple tools that share a common interoperable data model (e.g., awk, grep, sed, etc.) to build solutions.

Figure 3-2 is the representation[3] of a complex molecule. If you happen to know this molecule, you either studied chemistry or you are a very happy person.[4]

---

3. No, you will not catch me on that. I was born in the country of Magritte, after all!

4. Its CAS number is 54910-89-3.

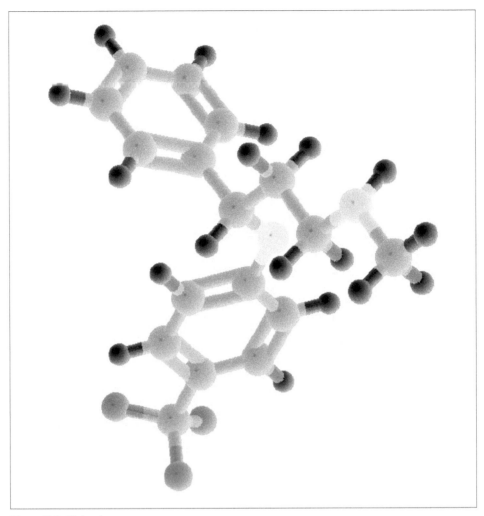

Figure 3-2. Molecule

The chemical formula of the molecule is $C_{17}H_{18}F_3NO$. With a mere 5 (common) elements from the 118 (at the moment) that the periodic table has, a molecule that saves lives every day was created!

Now, chemistry is slightly more complex than throwing elements together, or a lot of people would be producing the above molecule at home. So let us stop the simile[5] here and take a look at ROC. How many elements does it contain? How easy is it to put them together? Can anybody do that?

---

5. Lego would be an even better simile, but I could not immediately find an example of a Lego creation saving a life.

The ROC equivalent of a periodic table element is of course a *resource*. The result of the composition of resources is once more a *resource*. It would seem that we are running out of vocabulary.

At the bottom of the resource food chain are the atomary resources. This is where— the horror—coding comes in. These resources and tools need to be written. However, if you make them well and keep them atomary. you will find that over time you write less and less of them. Very little business logic should find its way to this level.

 To stress the atomary aspect, take the Unix *ls* tool. Would this be a *perfect* candidate? No! Why not? It should not do anything beyond list- ing the contents of a directory. The filtering and pretty-printing and . . . that you can invoke through switches, should not be in the *ls* tool itself. It would be a *good* candidate though.

Composing tools is next, for yes, at some level, anybody (who knows the problem) can do the composing. It just depends on the abstraction level of the tools. This is the stage in which a developer-architect or architect-developer team composes the tools that will build the system. With each new level of abstraction, more and more business logic will seep in, but care should be taken to keep it at a minimum (as reusability has an inverse relation to it).

Composing the information system itself is a task for the architect-enduser or enduser-architect team. At this level business logic is what it is all about.

Finally, the constraints are put upon the system, another task for the developer-archi- tect team.

Conclusion

You should leave this chapter with the feeling that there is a lot more to ROC than meets the eye, and that the foundations are (ROC) solid. Remember the "What is NetKernel?"-question from Chapter 1? Try answering it now!

CHAPTER 4

Humongous Fun

NoSQL is hot. Can NetKernel join in the fray? Yes, it can, and this chapter shows you how easy that is.

Background

The Internet is awash with (often Open Source) initiatives that cover the full range of IT, and beyond. Personally, I love it. When I go browsing without a goal, there is no telling what I will find (another reason for always having a goal upfront). Most such pet projects are short-lived. Some might be interesting, but the available information or documentation is usually so absent that I don't bother. Now and then, something catches my fancy.

MongoDB caught my eye because it is positioned as a good database backend for a logging application. I wrote one of those (a logging application, that is) myself, and typically these are the issues involved:

- Not fast enough
- Not flexible enough (schema-wise)
- Not flexible enough (search-option-wise)

Here is my personal thought on the first issue: If it is for logging the occasional error you introduce, how fast do you expect it to be when you are sequentially processing a file containing 2 million lines on a 4 quadcore 64 Mb machine? What if, on top of that, you log the whole line and five informational loggings for each line in the file? Oh, and did I mention the 5,000 end users using the same logging application for their online processing? They would like to get some work done today, too. By the way, do you know what the storage on the logging database is going to cost you on a monthly basis?[1]

The flexibility issue is harder to knock down. There are some fixed fields in all loggings, but having those and one big, unmanageable, unindexable, and thus unsearchable

---

1. Forgive me the rant.

message field is not a good solution. And what is the point of having tons of loggings (good question) if you are not able to mine, slice, and dice them?

There are of course solutions to the issues. Most relational databases now have text-indexing and text-search engines (Oracle Text springs to mind). And then there are engines like Lucene (in fact, Lucene is one of the batteries included in NetKernel).

Still, how quickly could I design an interface for MongoDB in NetKernel? Or—to put it less as a pet project of my own—say my company decides tomorrow to move to MongoDB; how quickly am I ready to roll?

MongoDB in Five Minutes

This is a book about NetKernel, so I am not going to have an installation guide for MongoDB in it. The website (*http://www.mongodb.org/*) contains all the information, and trust me, you'll be up and running an instance in five minutes (on Linux or on Windows, you choose); it is that simple.

 All right, all right, just the one hint. A very common (so I'm told) mistake is forgetting that the default location for the database files usually does not exist. You should always first create a location (choose your own) and then start the database as follows:

```
mongod --dbpath /path/to/location
```

 This chapter has been written with MongoDB release 1.8.2. It has been re-verified for MongoDB release 2.0.1. Intermediate releases should work without a problem as well, but they have not been verified.

Document Database

Forget Codd for now. It's all very nice, entities and relationships and normalization, but that does not help a lot when what you want is to store web pages and make them easily retrievable and searchable.

Let us compare a relational database to a document database.

Relational database	Document database
database	database
entity	collection
record	document

No, it is not just a matter of different names. A document can be an entire web page, whereas a record (or row) obviously can not. A collection groups documents that are alike (in a very broad sense), whereas an entity (or table) groups records with the exact same structure.

Also, add *laziness*. If you insert into a nonexisting collection after connecting to a nonexisting database, both database and collection will be created for you as needed. This makes things, as we'll see, a lot easier.

Showtime

MongoDB is very JavaScript minded and every installation comes with a JavaScript command-line interface (check the documentation to see how you start it).

Example 4-1. MongoDB in action - 1

```
MongoDB shell version: 1.8.2
connecting to: test
> use loggingdb
switched to db loggingdb
> db.loggings.insert({
... 'log':"NETKERNEL", 'logarea':"APPLICATION",
... 'severity':6,'facility':1,
... 'logging':"Started First Module"})
> db.loggings.find()
{ "_id" : ObjectId("4e0b64dfae7c0689d27b31fb"),
  "log" : "NETKERNEL", "logarea" : "APPLICATION",
  "severity" : 6, "facility" : 1,
  "logging" : "Started First Module"}
>
```

 The *ellipses* are not part of the insert syntax; they are provided by the JavaScript command-line interface to indicate a line continuation.

That wasn't very hard, was it? You can deduce that I inserted one document (a logging, actually) into the *loggings* collection of the *loggingdb* database, and found it again, too. I did not create either database or collection beforehand, and the layout of the document is from my own (relational) logging database.

Now, the network team wants an extra attribute in their loggings (since these always come from a network device). That is possible:

Example 4-2. MongoDB in action - 2

```
> db.loggings.insert({
... 'log':"NETWORK",'logarea':"SWITCHES",
... 'severity':6,'facility':1,
... 'logging':"Device rebooted",
... 'device':'evilcoreswitch'})
> db.loggings.find()
{ "_id" : ObjectId("4e0b64dfae7c0689d27b31fb"),
```

```
      "log" : "NETKERNEL", "logarea" : "APPLICATION",
      "severity" : 6, "facility" : 1,
      "logging" : "Started First Module"}
{ "_id" : ObjectId("4e0b681eae7c0689d27b31fc"),
      "log" : "NETWORK", "logarea" : "SWITCHES",
      "severity" : 6, "facility" : 1,
      "logging" : "Device rebooted",
      "device" : "evilcoreswitch" }
>
```

And so on and so on. Extensive querying is possible, limited only by your imagination and your *JSON* (see below) knowledge. From my limited testing, I'd say the flexibility issue moves back from the database to the application. A serious study of MongoDB is definitely on my to-do list.

That, however, is the topic of another book. Right now the goal is to create a MongoDB interface in NetKernel.

 JavaScript Object Notation is, like XML, a human-readable data format, closely related to JavaScript. Applications that use JavaScript on the client end will often use it for data handling because it translates into a JavaScript object easily. For NetKernel, JSON is just one of many representation forms that it handles quite happily. MongoDB internally uses BSON (the binary form of JSON), and its interfaces use JSON.

Hammer Time—The Module

Before getting down to it, let's state up front what we are going to accomplish: "We are going to build a simple interface that will allow us to do insert, update, delete (remove), and select (find) actions on a MongoDB instance."

Design

I took the above goal and came up with the following requirements and limitations:[2]

- We are building an interface, a library, which will hopefully be used in many other applications. It's ideal to introduce a second pattern, "The Service Accessor" pattern.[3]

- A grammar will handle the requests and pass them on to Groovy-script handlers (one for each action). Yes, I know that I was going to avoid using a lot of different languages, but the MongoDB drivers come in several flavors (DPML not among them), and Groovy is preinstalled in NetKernel (it is extensively used in NetKernel itself, as a complement to Java). So I use the driver from the *jar*.

---

2. The limitations are not due to NetKernel, they are due to me wanting to keep this section within limits.

3. The first one was "The Web Server" pattern.

- Our requests will be simple fire-and-forget requests. By that I mean they will start out stateless, make their own connection, do their thing, clean up their own connection, and return their result.
- MongoDB allows for easy replication and high availability. Use of either of those is outside the scope of this module. The database server in the request will look like *hostname:portname*, for example, localhost:27017, or *ip:portname*, for example, 192.168.1.10:27017.

Given all that, here's the module definition I came up with:

Example 4-3. [moduleroot]/module.xml

```
<?xml version="1.0" encoding="UTF-8"?>
<module version="2.0">
  <meta>
    <identity>
      <uri>urn:org:netkernelbook:chapter4:mongodb</uri>
      <version>1.0.0</version>
    </identity>
    <info>
      <name>MongoDB Database Tools</name>
      <description>Netkernelbook Chapter 4 MongoDB Database Tools</description>
    </info>
  </meta>

  <system>
    <dynamic/>
  </system>

  <rootspace
    name="MongoDB Database Tools"
    public="true"
    uri="urn:org:netkernelbook:chapter4:mongodb">
    <mapper>
      <config>
        <endpoint>
          <id>mongodb:interfaceEP</id>
          <name>MongoDB Database Tools - Interface</name>
          <description>MongoDB Database Tools - Interface</description>
          <grammar>
            <active>
              <identifier>active:mongodb</identifier>
              <argument name="databaseserver" min="1" max="1"
                desc="[server:port] combination,
                for example localhost:27017"/>
              <argument name="databasename" min="1" max="1"
                desc="[name] of the database to connect to,
                e.g. loggingdb"/>
              <argument name="collectionname" min="1" max="1"
                desc="[name] of the collection,
                e.g. loggings"/>
              <argument name="action" min="1" max="1"
                desc="[action] to be performed, valid are count,
                insert, update, delete, select and drop"/>
```

```
              <varargs/>
            </active>
          </grammar>
          <request>
            <identifier>active:groovy</identifier>
            <argument name="operator">
              res:/resources/endpoints/mongodb_[[arg:action]].groovy
            </argument>
            <argument method="as-string" name="databaseserver">
              arg:databaseserver
            </argument>
            <argument method="as-string" name="databasename">
              arg:databasename
            </argument>
            <argument method="as-string" name="collectionname">
              arg:collectionname
            </argument>
            <varargs/>
          </request>
        </endpoint>
      </config>

      <space>
        <fileset>
          <regex>res:/resources/endpoints/mongodb_(insert|update|delete|select|
drop).groovy</regex>
          <private />
        </fileset>
        <fileset>
          <private />
          <regex>res:/lib/.*</regex>
        </fileset>
        <import>
          <private />
          <uri>urn:org:netkernel:lang:groovy</uri>
        </import>
        <import>
          <private />
          <uri>urn:org:netkernel:json:core</uri>
        </import>
      </space>
    </mapper>
  </rootspace>

  <rootspace
    name="MongoDB Database Tools - Documentation"
    public="true"
    uri="urn:org:netkernelbook:chapter4:mongodb:documentation">
    <fileset>
      <regex>res:/etc/system/(Books|Docs).xml</regex>
    </fileset>
    <fileset>
      <regex>res:/resources/documentation/.*</regex>
    </fileset>
  </rootspace>
```

```
<rootspace
    name="MongoDB Database Tools - Unit Test"
    public="true"
    uri="urn:org:netkernelbook:chapter4:mongodb:unittest">
    <fileset>
        <regex>res:/etc/system/Tests.xml</regex>
    </fileset>
    <fileset>
        <regex>res:/resources/unittest/.*</regex>
    </fileset>

    <endpoint>
        <prototype>Limiter</prototype>
        <grammar>res:/etc/
            <regex type="anything"/>
        </grammar>
    </endpoint>

    <import>
        <uri>urn:org:netkernelbook:chapter4:mongodb</uri>
    </import>

    <import>
        <uri>urn:org:netkernel:lang:groovy</uri>
    </import>
    <import>
        <uri>urn:org:netkernel:json:core</uri>
    </import>
    <import>
        <private/>
        <uri>urn:org:netkernel:ext:layer1</uri>
    </import>
</rootspace>
</module>
```

No Dynamic Export

The first thing to notice in the *[moduleroot]/module.xml* file is the absence of a *Simple-DynamicImportHook.xml*. After a while, you get so used to common "patterns" that you forget what they were for in the first place. Remember that it's a library we are writing here, a library to be used in other applications. Exposing it to the Frontend (or Backend) HTTPFulcrum is unnecessary and a potential security risk.

As a consequence, we'll require another application to use this one. But not to worry, the *Xunit Test* application will do fine. And our *[moduleroot]/module.xml* has a root-space for that.

Grammar

We only have a single entry point, so actually our *[moduleroot]/module.xml* does not differ all that much from the *First Module* one. The tricky part is getting the grammar right. Let's take another look at it:

Example 4-4. Active grammar

```
<grammar>
  <active>
    <identifier>active:mongodb</identifier>
    <argument name="databaseserver" min="1" max="1"/>
    <argument name="databasename" min="1" max="1"/>
    <argument name="collectionname" min="1" max="1"/>
    <argument name="action" min="1" max="1"/>
    <varargs/>
  </active>
</grammar>
```

Admit it, that is impressive. But did the above spring from my mind in one piece (like Athena sprang full grown, spear, helmet, and all, from Zeus's head)?[4]It did not.

Grammar's Kitchen

At last, here's another visit to the Backend HTTPFulcrum, and straight to the kitchen, too! Seriously, the Backend HTTPFulcrum is in itself a showcase for NetKernel and contains a number of powerful tools. So why do I not focus on them?

Well, at one point in time, a friend of mine bought a house with a big garden and wanted the trees removed from said garden. So we got ourselves equipped with every imaginable tree cutting/pruning/chopping/sawing tool and went at it. On our first tree (little more than a shoot that had been going strong for a year or four, maybe only three), we spent most of a day, going through four chains on the chainsaw and coming close to destroying a neighbor's shed as well as losing a limb or two.

We learned every lesson on tree chopping, the hard way. But we were lucky, and a week later, we cut down branches the size of that original shoot from 50-year-old trees in seconds. And they fell (from up to 8 meters high) where we wanted them to fall. We left the big naked trunks for the real professionals. Yes, we learned that lesson, too (basic geometry: if it is 10 meters high standing up, it can reach 10 meters far crashing down).

Before I'm handing you tools, you'll know what to do with them, and trust me, we'll cover most of the Backend HTTPFulcrum tools before this book is through. *Grammar's Kitchen*[5] is where we are heading now:

---

4. This happened in Greek mythology. Afterward, Zeus became the lead singer for Fischer-Z (hence the Z) and wrote the song "Pretty Paracetamol," or something along those lines.

Figure 4-1. Simple active URI grammar

- Start *your favorite web browser.*
- Browse to *http://localhost:1060/tools/grammar.*

As you can see, the documentation is on the right. On the left, you can experiment with a grammar, enter an identifier, and check to see if it matches. At the bottom, there's a *Cookbook* with a couple of examples. To start our own grammar, select the *Simple active URI grammar* example (from the *Active Grammars* submenu). See Figure 4-1.

You probably deduced that when you select the Parse Identifier button, the grammar is applied to the identifier. Select it after each step we take so you can see how the grammar is being built up.

Example 4-5. Building our grammar, step 1

Grammar:
```
<grammar>
  <active>
    <identifier>active:mongodb</identifier>
    <argument name="action" min="1" max="1"/>
  </active>
</grammar>
```

Identifier:
```
active:mongodb
```

Did you select the Parse Identifier button? Then you noticed our identifier did not match the grammar, right? Good! The reason is that we made the action argument mandatory

---

5. Nothing to do with Gordon Ramsay (if that name does not ring a bell . . . keep it that way), it's a pun on Grandma's Kitchen.

(min="1", max="1"). If we had made it optional (min="0", max="1") our identifier would have worked. Try that! OK? Now, make it mandatory again, and let's change the identifier.

Example 4-6. Building our grammar, step 2

Identifier:
```
active:mongodb+action@insert
```

Let's add the rest of the mandatory arguments in one go.

Example 4-7. Building our grammar, step 3

Grammar:
```
<grammar>
  <active>
    <identifier>active:mongodb</identifier>
    <argument name="databaseserver" min="1" max="1"/>
    <argument name="databasename" min="1" max="1"/>
    <argument name="collectionname" min="1" max="1"/>
    <argument name="action" min="1" max="1"/>
  </active>
</grammar>
```

Identifier:
```
active:mongodb+action@insert
+databaseserver@localhost:27070
+databasename@loggingdb
+collectionname@loggings
```

The above arguments are valid for every type of action. Depending on the action, however, there may be (at least) one or more other arguments. There are two ways to resolve this. Either we specify all possible arguments as optional, or we get lazy (as I did).

Example 4-8. Building our grammar, step 4

Grammar:
```
<grammar>
  <active>
    <identifier>active:mongodb</identifier>
    <argument name="databaseserver" min="1" max="1"/>
    <argument name="databasename" min="1" max="1"/>
    <argument name="collectionname" min="1" max="1"/>
    <argument name="action" min="1" max="1"/>
    <varargs/>
  </active>
</grammar>
```

Both the following identifiers will now resolve correctly. Try *them* yourself (Figure 4-2), and come up with some of your own:

Example 4-9. Building our grammar, step 5

Identifier:
```
active:mongodb+action@insert
+databaseserver@localhost:27070
+databasename@loggingdb
+collectionname@loggings
+docs@[{'log':"NETKERNEL", 'logarea':"APPLICATION",
       'severity':5, 'facility':2,
       'logging':"Run of MongoDB Multi Insert 1",
       'application' : "MongoDB Interface"},
      {'log':"NETKERNEL", 'logarea':"APPLICATION",
       'severity':5,'facility':2,
       'logging':"Run of MongoDB Multi Insert 2",
       'application' : "MongoDB Interface"}]
```

Identifier:
```
active:mongodb+action@find
+databaseserver@localhost:27070
+databasename@loggingdb
+collectionname@loggings
+criteria@{}
+fields@{}
```

Pretty nifty tool, is it not? You'll use it quite often. In fact, I use it for something that is not strictly NetKernel related, too.

Example 4-10. Grammar's Kitchen—RegEx

Grammar:
```
<grammar><regex>[A-Z].{2}[A-Z].{5}</regex></grammar>
```

Identifier:
```
NetKernel
```

Regular Expressions are a pain in the nether regions, and yet they are everywhere in IT. In Grammar's Kitchen, you can write them and test them without having to write a single line of code.

Request

With the grammar covered, the request part of our endpoint is pretty straightforward.

Example 4-11. Request

```
<request>
  <identifier>active:groovy</identifier>
  <argument name="operator">
    res:/resources/endpoints/mongodb_[[arg:action]].groovy
  </argument>
  <argument method="as-string" name="databaseserver">
    arg:databaseserver
  </argument>
  <argument method="as-string" name="databasename">
```

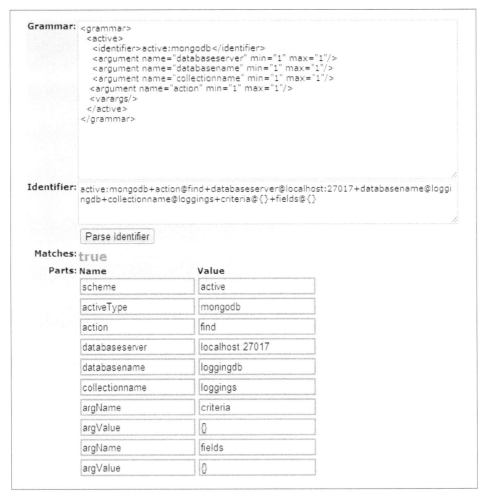

Grammar:
```
<grammar>
  <active>
    <identifier>active:mongodb</identifier>
    <argument name="databaseserver" min="1" max="1"/>
    <argument name="databasename" min="1" max="1"/>
    <argument name="collectionname" min="1" max="1"/>
    <argument name="action" min="1" max="1"/>
    <varargs/>
  </active>
</grammar>
```

Identifier: active:mongodb+action@find+databaseserver@localhost:27017+databasename@loggingdb+collectionname@loggings+criteria@{}+fields@{}

[Parse Identifier]

Matches: true

Parts:

Name	Value
scheme	active
activeType	mongodb
action	find
databaseserver	localhost:27017
databasename	loggingdb
collectionname	loggings
argName	criteria
argValue	{}
argName	fields
argValue	{}

Figure 4-2. Parsed grammar

```
    arg:databasename
  </argument>
  <argument method="as-string" name="collectionname">
    arg:collectionname
  </argument>
  <varargs/>
</request>
```

Well, maybe it is not straightforward. There are three ways to add an argument to a request:

1. *As a reference.* The operator argument above is an example. We are passing a reference (its URI, as a string) of the resource. Argument substitutions can be used to make this more dynamic.

```
<argument name="operator">
  res:/resources/groovy/mongodb_[[arg:action]].groovy
</argument>
```

2. *As a value.* We pass in a literal. No argument substitutions can be used (it's a literal . . . no substitutions, exchanges, or refunds).

```
<argument name="logonid">
  <literal type="string">mylogonid</literal>
</argument>
```

3. *As a request.* The request can itself contain a child request element.

```
<argument name="logonid">
  <request>
    <identifier>active:determineRandomLogonid</identifier>
  </request>
</argument>
```

You can probably see the problem. We need to pass values (a database name is not a reference to a resource), but these are not literals. We get them from argument substitution.

By using the method attribute, we can override the default behaviour. The *as-string* means that we have an incoming pass-by reference (the arguments extracted from our grammar) that we want to turn into a pass-by value. Note that we could also leave the method override out and specify the following (example for database server):

```
<argument name="databaseserver">
  data:text/plain,[[arg:databaseserver]]
</argument>
```

In this way, you do have a reference to a resource, and you can thus use the vanilla way as a reference. Personally, I find the method override to be clearer, but whatever works best for you is fine.

The Driver

Before tackling the actual Groovy code, we are going to need the MongoDB driver. You can find the java driver at *https://github.com/mongodb/mongo-java-driver/archives/master*. At the time of this writing, this is mongo-2.6.3.jar. You should drop this in the *[moduleroot]/lib* directory of your module.

 Why put this in the lib subdirectory? Search for *classloader* in the Back-end HTTPFulcrum search tool (http://localhost:1060/tools/search/) and you'll find (in the first hit) where NetKernel searches for classes (and in what order those locations are visited).

 If you're not finding anything, you might need to (re)build your Search Index first (http://localhost:1060/tools/search/fullIndex).

Insert

From the grammar, you can deduce that we are going to have several Groovy programs, one for each action. Let's start with *insert*.

Example 4-12. [moduleroot]/resources/endpoints/mongodb_insert.groovy

```groovy
import com.mongodb.*;
import com.mongodb.util.*;
import org.json.*;

// Prepare the result
jsonResult = new JSONObject();
jsonResult.put("success",true);
jsonResult.put("errors",[]);
jsonResult.put("message",'');

// No errorchecking needed for the following three arguments,
// our grammar takes care of them.
databaseserver = context.source("arg:databaseserver", String.class);
databasename = context.source("arg:databasename", String.class);
collectionname = context.source("arg:collectionname", String.class);

// Get the docs argument. Its either a valid JSONObject or a
// valid JSONArray. Exceptions are caught.
docs = null;

try{
  docs = context.source("arg:docs", JSONObject.class);
}
catch(eo){
  try{
    docs = context.source("arg:docs", JSONArray.class);
  }
  catch(ea){
    jsonResult.putOpt("success",false);
    jsonResult.putOpt("message","Argument docs is missing or incorrect");
  }
}

if ((docs != null)){
  try {
    mConnection = new Mongo(databaseserver);
    mDatabase   = mConnection.getDB(databasename);
    mCollection = mDatabase.getCollection(collectionname);

    insertresult = mCollection.insert(JSON.parse(docs.toString()));
    if (insertresult.getLastError().ok()){
      if (insertresult.getError()){
        jsonResult.putOpt("success",false);
        jsonResult.putOpt("message",insertresult.getError());
      }
      else {
        jsonResult.putOpt("message","Insert is succesful");
      }
```

```
      }
      else {
        jsonResult.putOpt("success",false);
        jsonResult.putOpt("message",
          insertresult.getLastError().getErrorMessage());
      }
      mConnection.close();
    }
    catch(e){
      if (mConnection){
        mConnection.close();
      }
      jsonResult.putOpt("success",false);
      jsonResult.putOpt("message","Insert failed on Mongo database");
    }
}

response = context.createResponseFrom(jsonResult);
response.setMimeType('application/json');
response.setExpiry(response.EXPIRY_ALWAYS);
```

Nothing special about the above code:

- The imports come from the driver jar.
- Since JSON is the lingua franca for MongoDB, the response will be a JSONObject.
- One extra argument, docs, needs to be handled. It can be a JSONObject (for a single insert) or a JSONArray (for multiple inserts).
- The connection to the database is closed before we return the response since we are doing fire-and-forget actions.
- The response is immediately expired. I prefer no caching risks with databases (and MongoDB, from what little documentation I read, seems to be vulnerable to those).
- *The context object is your interface to the ROC world.* I didn't mention this in our *First Module.* DPML sort of shields you from it. In all other language implementations, you are handed a context object, which hands you full control over your request and full access to your request space (the NKF API, in other words). Don't worry if you can not see the power of that right now, in our small Groovy action programs, we use the context to get our arguments in and our response out.

Update

Next on the usual-database-action list is an *update.*

Example 4-13. [moduleroot]/resources/endpoints/mongodb_update.groovy

```
import com.mongodb.*;
import com.mongodb.util.*;
import org.json.*;

// Prepare the result
```

```
jsonResult = new JSONObject();
jsonResult.put("success",true);
jsonResult.put("errors",[]);
jsonResult.put("message",'');

// No errorchecking needed for the following three arguments,
// our grammar takes care of them.
databaseserver = context.source("arg:databaseserver", String.class);
databasename = context.source("arg:databasename", String.class);
collectionname = context.source("arg:collectionname", String.class);

// Get the criteria argument. It has to be a valid JSONObject.
criteria = null;

try{
  criteria = context.source("arg:criteria", JSONObject.class);
}
catch(ec){
  jsonResult.putOpt("success",false);
  jsonResult.putOpt("message",
    "Argument criteria is missing or incorrect");
}

// Get the objNew argument. It has to be a valid JSONObject.
objNew = null;

try{
  objNew = context.source("arg:objNew", JSONObject.class);
}
catch(eo){
  jsonResult.putOpt("success",false);
  jsonResult.putOpt("message","Argument objNew is missing or incorrect");
}

// Get the upsert argument. It has to be a valid Boolean.
upsert = null;

try{
  upsert = context.source("arg:upsert", Boolean.class);
}
catch(eu){
  jsonResult.putOpt("success",false);
  jsonResult.putOpt("message","Argument upsert is missing or incorrect");
}

// Get the multi argument. It has to be a valid Boolean.
multi = null;

try{
  multi = context.source("arg:multi", Boolean.class);
}
catch(em){
  jsonResult.putOpt("success",false);
  jsonResult.putOpt("message","Argument multi is missing or incorrect");
}
```

```
if ((criteria != null) &&
    (objNew != null) &&
    (upsert != null) &&
    (multi != null)){
  try {
    mConnection = new Mongo(databaseserver);
    mDatabase   = mConnection.getDB(databasename);
    mCollection = mDatabase.getCollection(collectionname);

    updateresult = mCollection.update(JSON.parse(criteria.toString()),
                                      JSON.parse(objNew.toString()),
                                      upsert,
                                      multi);
    if (updateresult.getLastError().ok()){
      if (updateresult.getError()){
        jsonResult.putOpt("success",false);
        jsonResult.putOpt("message",updateresult.getError());
      }
      else {
        jsonResult.putOpt("message","Update is succesful");
      }
    }
    else {
      jsonResult.putOpt("success",false);
      jsonResult.putOpt("message",
        updateresult.getLastError().getErrorMessage());
    }
    mConnection.close();
  }
  catch(e){
    if (mConnection){
      mConnection.close();
    }
    jsonResult.putOpt("success",false);
    jsonResult.putOpt("message","Update failed on Mongo database");
  }
}

response = context.createResponseFrom(jsonResult);
response.setMimeType('application/json');
response.setExpiry(response.EXPIRY_ALWAYS);
```

A couple more arguments are passed, but otherwise this is almost the same as the insert code. Let's move on quickly.

Delete

Delete is another must-have database action. The MongoDB command is in fact *remove*.

Example 4-14. [moduleroot]/resources/endpoints/mongodb_delete.groovy

```groovy
import com.mongodb.*;
import com.mongodb.util.*;
import org.json.*;

// Prepare the result
jsonResult = new JSONObject();
jsonResult.put("success",true);
jsonResult.put("errors",[]);
jsonResult.put("message",'');

// No errorchecking needed for the following three arguments,
// our grammar takes care of them.
databaseserver = context.source("arg:databaseserver", String.class);
databasename = context.source("arg:databasename", String.class);
collectionname = context.source("arg:collectionname", String.class);

// Get the criteria argument. It has to be a valid JSONObject.
criteria = null;

try{
  criteria = context.source("arg:criteria", JSONObject.class);
}
catch(ec){
  jsonResult.putOpt("success",false);
  jsonResult.putOpt("message",
    "Argument criteria is missing or incorrect");
}

if ((criteria != null)){
  try {
    mConnection = new Mongo(databaseserver);
    mDatabase   = mConnection.getDB(databasename);
    mCollection = mDatabase.getCollection(collectionname);

    deleteresult = mCollection.remove(JSON.parse(criteria.toString()));
    if (deleteresult.getLastError().ok()){
      if (deleteresult.getError()){
        jsonResult.putOpt("success",false);
        jsonResult.putOpt("message",deleteresult.getError());
      }
      else {
        jsonResult.putOpt("message","Delete is succesful");
      }
    }
    else {
      jsonResult.putOpt("success",false);
      jsonResult.putOpt("message",
        deleteresult.getLastError().getErrorMessage());
    }
    mConnection.close();
  }
  catch(e){
    if (mConnection){
      mConnection.close();
```

```
    }
    jsonResult.putOpt("success",false);
    jsonResult.putOpt("message","Delete failed on Mongo database");
  }
}

response = context.createResponseFrom(jsonResult);
response.setMimeType('application/json');
response.setExpiry(response.EXPIRY_ALWAYS);
```

Oh my, this is getting quite boring, is it not?

Select

Select is the most used database action ever. The MongoDB command is *find*.

Example 4-15. [moduleroot]/resources/endpoints/mongodb_delete.groovy
```
import com.mongodb.*;
import com.mongodb.util.*;
import org.json.*;

// Prepare the result
jsonResult = new JSONObject();
jsonResult.put("success",true);
jsonResult.put("errors",[]);
jsonResult.put("message",'');

// No errorchecking needed for the following three arguments,
// our grammar takes care of them.
databaseserver = context.source("arg:databaseserver", String.class);
databasename = context.source("arg:databasename", String.class);
collectionname = context.source("arg:collectionname", String.class);

// Get the criteria argument. It has to be a valid JSONObject.
criteria = null;

try{
  criteria = context.source("arg:criteria", JSONObject.class);
}
catch(ec){
  jsonResult.putOpt("success",false);
  jsonResult.putOpt("message",
    "Argument criteria is missing or incorrect");
}

fields = null;

try{
  fields = context.source("arg:fields", JSONObject.class);
}
catch(ef){
  jsonResult.putOpt("success",false);
  jsonResult.putOpt("message","Argument fields is missing or incorrect");
```

```
}

// Optional arguments ...

optskip = null;

try{
  optskip = context.source("arg:skip", Integer.class);
}
catch(es){
  optskip = 0;
}

optlimit = null;

try{
  optlimit = context.source("arg:limit", Integer.class);
}
catch(el){
  optlimit = 0;
}

optsort = null;
try{
  optsort = context.source("arg:sort", JSONObject.class);
}
catch(es){
  optsort = new JSONObject();
}

selectresult = null;

if ((criteria != null) &&
    (fields != null)){
  try {
    mConnection = new Mongo(databaseserver);
    mDatabase   = mConnection.getDB(databasename);
    mCollection = mDatabase.getCollection(collectionname);

    selectresult = new JSONArray();
    selectcursor = mCollection.find(
      JSON.parse(criteria.toString()),
      JSON.parse(fields.toString())
    ).sort(JSON.parse(optsort.toString())).skip(optskip).limit(optlimit);

    selectcursor.each{
      selectresult.put(new JSONObject(it.toString()));
    };
    mConnection.close();
  }
  catch(e){
    if (mConnection){
      mConnection.close();
    }
    jsonResult.putOpt("success",false);
```

```
      jsonResult.putOpt("message","The select failed on Mongo database");
   }
}

if (selectresult != null){
  response = context.createResponseFrom(selectresult);
}
else {
  response = context.createResponseFrom(jsonResult);
}
response.setMimeType('application/json');
response.setExpiry(response.EXPIRY_ALWAYS);
```

The code for the select is slightly (only slightly) more complex because it is useless to return whether or not it succeeded. You want to know what it found. Here's the technical lowdown:

- A MongoDB find returns a cursor to the result. We loop through this cursor, appending each result to a JSONArray. The response for a select will therefore always be a JSONArray, unless there is an issue with the database itself (in which case you get a JSONObject returned).
- There are five extra arguments here. With criteria, fields, skip, limit, and sort, you can make any query imaginable and do database paging in your application, if you want to.

Drop

Not one of the big four database actions, but useful nonetheless, is the *drop* action. In MongoDB, this drops a collection. It can be very useful if you've been experimenting, and since a collection is (re)created lazily at the first insert, there's no create action needed either.

Example 4-16. [moduleroot]/resources/endpoints/mongodb_drop.groovy

```
import com.mongodb.*;
import com.mongodb.util.*;
import org.json.*;

// Prepare the result
jsonResult = new JSONObject();
jsonResult.put("success",true);
jsonResult.put("errors",[]);
jsonResult.put("message",'');

// No errorchecking needed for the following three arguments,
// our grammar takes care of them.
databaseserver = context.source("arg:databaseserver", String.class);
databasename = context.source("arg:databasename", String.class);
collectionname = context.source("arg:collectionname", String.class);

try {
```

```
  mConnection = new Mongo(databaseserver);
  mDatabase   = mConnection.getDB(databasename);
  mCollection = mDatabase.getCollection(collectionname);

  mCollection.drop();

  jsonResult.putOpt("message","Drop is succesful");

  mConnection.close();
}
catch(e){
  if (mConnection){
    mConnection.close();
  }
  jsonResult.putOpt("success",false);
  jsonResult.putOpt("message","The drop failed on Mongo database");
}


response = context.createResponseFrom(jsonResult);
response.setMimeType('application/json');
response.setExpiry(response.EXPIRY_ALWAYS);
```

Count

This action was not in my original set, but an application I was doing required it. When you want to implement database paging in your application, you'll need it, too.

Example 4-17. [moduleroot]/resources/endpoints/mongodb_count.groovy

```
import com.mongodb.*;
import com.mongodb.util.*;
import org.json.*;

// Prepare the result
jsonResult = new JSONObject();
jsonResult.put("success",true);
jsonResult.put("errors",[]);
jsonResult.put("message",'');

// No errorchecking needed for the following three arguments,
// our grammar takes care of them.
databaseserver = context.source("arg:databaseserver", String.class);
databasename = context.source("arg:databasename", String.class);
collectionname = context.source("arg:collectionname", String.class);

// Get the criteria argument. It has to be a valid JSONObject.
criteria = null;

try{
  criteria = context.source("arg:criteria", JSONObject.class);
}
catch(ec){
  jsonResult.putOpt("success",false);
```

```
    jsonResult.putOpt("message",
      "Argument criteria is missing or incorrect");
}

countresult = null;

if ((criteria != null)){
  try {
    mConnection = new Mongo(databaseserver);
    mDatabase   = mConnection.getDB(databasename);
    mCollection = mDatabase.getCollection(collectionname);

    cursorcount = mCollection.find(
      JSON.parse(criteria.toString())
    ).count();

    countresult = new JSONObject();
    countresult.put("totalcount",cursorcount);

    mConnection.close();
  }
  catch(e){
    if (mConnection){
      mConnection.close();
    }
    jsonResult.putOpt("success",false);
    jsonResult.putOpt("message","The count failed on Mongo database");
  }
}

if (countresult != null){
  response = context.createResponseFrom(countresult);
}
else {
  response = context.createResponseFrom(jsonResult);
}
response.setMimeType('application/json');
response.setExpiry(response.EXPIRY_ALWAYS);
```

Missing in Action

Are the above six the only possible actions on a MongoDB database? No, but they are
the most important. *Creating an index* was the next one on my list; I leave that one up
to you.

Testing

Our module is now up and running, but so far you've only got my word for it that it
does anything at all. Since it is not available on the Frontend HTTPFulcrum, there's
no easy way to test it. Right? Well, actually, there are two ways. Both are in the Backend
HTTPFulcrum:

- XUnit Testing—http://localhost:1060/test/
- Request Resolution trace tool—http://localhost:1060/tools/requesttrace

 I've put testing in a separate subsection, not because it is something *separate*, but because I can give it the attention it deserves that way. When you develop an application, writing code and writing tests go hand in glove.

 A running MongoDB instance is required for the tests below. I'm running it on the same machine where NetKernel is running, so *localhost: 27017* is where my database server can be found. Adapt the examples to your configuration where necessary.

Before we get into the details for both, there's one thing that I have to clear up beforehand. It's about the *optional arguments*. Remember that we ensured that the mandatory arguments will all be passed as strings to the request? Well, since we didn't specify a similar thing for all the optional parameters (because I was lazy, I admit it), we will have to deal with it now. So, if you notice the difference (and you should) between the passing of the mandatory and the optional arguments, the reason is my earlier laziness.

 By all means, go back and extend the grammar with all possible optional arguments. Then come back here and remove the extra stuff from the tests that follow.

In order to push our module into *XUnit Testing*, we require a *Tests.xml* file.

Example 4-18. [moduleroot]/etc/system/Tests.xml

```xml
<?xml version="1.0" encoding="UTF-8"?>
<tests>
  <test>
    <id>test:urn:org:netkernelbook:chapter4:mongodb</id>
    <name>MongoDB Database Tools - Unit Test</name>
    <desc>netkernelbook chapter4 mongodb database tools unittest</desc>
    <uri>res:/resources/unittest/testlist.xml</uri>
  </test>
</tests>
```

This little more than suggests the next file we have to take a look at.

Example 4-19. [moduleroot]/resources/unittest/testlist.xml

```xml
<?xml version="1.0" encoding="UTF-8"?>
<testlist>

  <assertDefinition name="validMongoDBaction">
    <identifier>active:groovy</identifier>
```

```
      <argument name="operator">
        res:/resources/unittest/validMongoDBaction.groovy
      </argument>
      <argument name="result">arg:test:result</argument>
      <argument name="validMongoDBaction">arg:test:tagValue</argument>
   </assertDefinition>

   <test name="Invoke service by identifier - insert action">
      <request>
        <identifier>active:mongodb</identifier>
        <argument name="databaseserver">localhost:27017</argument>
        <argument name="databasename">loggingdb</argument>
        <argument name="collectionname">loggings</argument>
        <argument name="action">insert</argument>
        <argument name="docs">
           <literal type="string">
[{'log':"NETKERNEL",
 'logarea':"APPLICATION",
 'severity':5,
 'facility':2,
 'logging':"Run of MongoDB Multi Insert 1",
 'application' : "MongoDB Interface"
},
{'log':"NETKERNEL",
 'logarea':"APPLICATION",
 'severity':5,
 'facility':2,
 'logging':"Run of MongoDB Multi Insert 2",
 'application' : "MongoDB Interface"
}
]
           </literal>
         </argument>
      </request>

      <assert>
        <validMongoDBaction>insert</validMongoDBaction>
      </assert>
   </test>

   <test name="Invoke service by identifier - update action">
      <request>
        <identifier>active:mongodb</identifier>
        <argument name="databaseserver">localhost:27017</argument>
        <argument name="databasename">loggingdb</argument>
        <argument name="collectionname">loggings</argument>
        <argument name="action">update</argument>
        <argument name="criteria">
          <literal type="string">
            {'log':"NETKERNEL"}
          </literal>
        </argument>
        <argument name="objNew">
          <literal type="string">
            {'$set':{'severity':4}}
```

```
        </literal>
      </argument>
      <argument name="upsert">
        <literal type="boolean">
          false
        </literal>
      </argument>
      <argument name="multi">
        <literal type="boolean">
          false
        </literal>
      </argument>
    </request>

    <assert>
      <validMongoDBaction>update</validMongoDBaction>
    </assert>
  </test>

  <test name="Invoke service by identifier - delete action">
    <request>
      <identifier>active:mongodb</identifier>
      <argument name="databaseserver">localhost:27017</argument>
      <argument name="databasename">loggingdb</argument>
      <argument name="collectionname">loggings</argument>
      <argument name="action">delete</argument>
      <argument name="criteria">
        <literal type="string">
          {'severity':4}
        </literal>
      </argument>
    </request>

    <assert>
      <validMongoDBaction>delete</validMongoDBaction>
    </assert>
  </test>

  <test name="Invoke service by identifier - select action">
    <request>
      <identifier>active:mongodb</identifier>
      <argument name="databaseserver">localhost:27017</argument>
      <argument name="databasename">loggingdb</argument>
      <argument name="collectionname">loggings</argument>
      <argument name="action">select</argument>
      <argument name="criteria">
        <literal type="string">
          {}
        </literal>
      </argument>
      <argument name="fields">
        <literal type="string">
          {}
        </literal>
      </argument>
```

```
      </request>

      <assert>
        <validMongoDBaction>select</validMongoDBaction>
      </assert>
  </test>

  <test name="Invoke service by identifier - count action">
    <request>
      <identifier>active:mongodb</identifier>
      <argument name="databaseserver">localhost:27017</argument>
      <argument name="databasename">loggingdb</argument>
      <argument name="collectionname">loggings</argument>
      <argument name="action">count</argument>
      <argument name="criteria">
        <literal type="string">
          {}
        </literal>
      </argument>
    </request>

    <assert>
      <validMongoDBaction>count</validMongoDBaction>
    </assert>
  </test>

  <test name="Invoke service by identifier - drop action">
    <request>
      <identifier>active:mongodb</identifier>
      <argument name="databaseserver">localhost:27017</argument>
      <argument name="databasename">loggingdb</argument>
      <argument name="collectionname">loggings</argument>
      <argument name="action">drop</argument>
    </request>

    <assert>
      <validMongoDBaction>drop</validMongoDBaction>
    </assert>
  </test>
</testlist>
```

That's quite a listing or better yet, that's quite an interesting listing. Each of our MongoDB actions has a test (exactly as it should be if you develop correctly) that can run independently or as a series. The first thing to notice is the construction for the optional arguments:

```
<argument name="criteria">
  <literal type="string">
  {'log':"NETKERNEL"}
  </literal>
</argument>
```

With the help of the literal tag, we enforce the fact that the data we pass is a value, not a reference, to a resource.

The second thing worthy of study is the fact that I use a *custom assert*. By all means, read up on the built-in asserts in the documentation, but our MongoDB library returns one of the following:

- For a valid select, a JSONArray containing the result set
- For a valid select/count, the result is not a status, but the actual data or a number. In all other cases, the result is a status (a JSONObject containing success or failure)
- For an valid count, a JSONObject containing a number

While you could certainly construct something with the built-in asserts, I decided to go with a custom assert.

Example 4-20. [moduleroot]/resources/unittest/validMongoDBaction.groovy

```
import org.json.*;

validMongoDBaction = null;
resultIn        = null;
resultOut       = true;

try{
  validMongoDBaction = context.source("arg:validMongoDBaction")
}
catch(e){
  resultOut = false;
}

try{
  resultIn = context.source("arg:result")
}
catch(e){
  resultOut = false;
}

if ((resultIn != null) &&
    (validMongoDBaction != null)){
  switch (validMongoDBaction) {
    case "insert" :
    case "update" :
    case "delete" :
    case "drop" :
      if (resultIn.has("success")){
        resultOut = resultIn.getBoolean("success");
      }
      else {
        resultOut = false;
      }
      break
    case "select" :
      if (resultIn instanceof JSONArray){
        resultOut = true;
        // println resultIn.getClass()
      }
```

```
    else{
      resultOut = false;
    }
    break;
  case "count" :
    if (resultIn.has("totalcount")){
      resultOut = true;
      // println resultIn.getLong("totalcount");
    }
    else{
      resultOut = false;
    }
    break
  default :
    resultOut = false;
  }
}

response = context.createResponseFrom(resultOut);
response.setMimeType('text/plain');
response.setExpiry(response.EXPIRY_ALWAYS);
```

Our custom assert is written in Groovy and manipulates JSONArrays and JSONObjects. In order to make this work, our unit test rootspace requires two imports that you may have wondered about.

```
<import>
  <uri>urn:org:netkernel:lang:groovy</uri>
</import>
<import>
  <uri>urn:org:netkernel:json:core</uri>
</import>
```

If you perform the tests one by one and check the MongoDB database (with the default client) in between, you'll be able to follow along. Still, it's pretty boring to have to do tests in order to actually *do* something on that database, no?

The Request Resolution Trace Tool comes to your rescue (see Figure 4-3)!

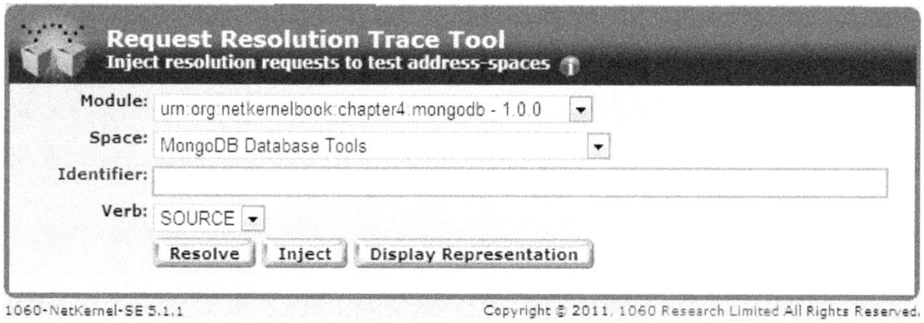

Figure 4-3. Request Resolution Trace Tool

This is a very powerful tool. It allows you to check the resolution of a request against a specific space. Let's see what the following identifier can teach us about it.

```
active:mongodb
+databaseserver@localhost:27017
+databasename@loggingdb
+collectionname@loggings
+action@drop
```

 The whole identifier has to be specified on one line, something that is rather impossible in a book.

You can see the result of a *Resolve* in Figure 4-4 and how an *Inject* actually executes the request in Figure 4-5.

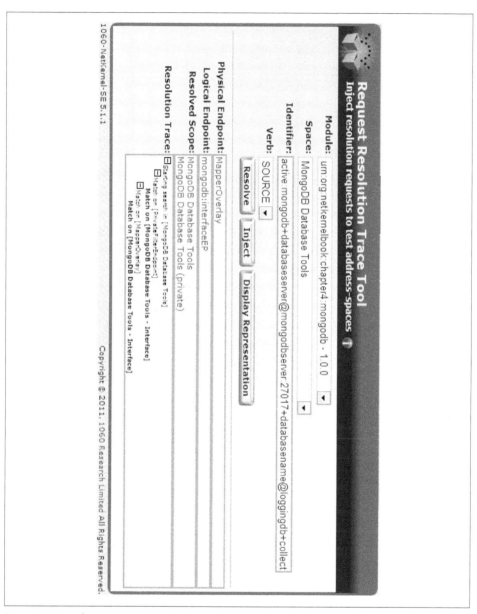

Figure 4-4. Resolve action

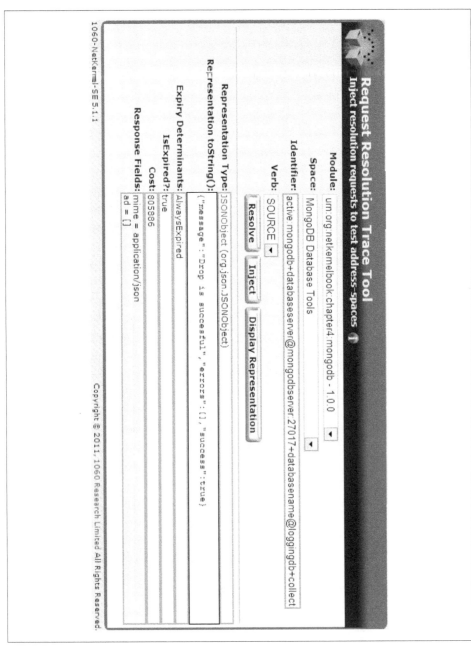

Figure 4-5. Inject action

Right, that should keep you happy for a while. Make sure to do a couple of *inserts*, experiment with the *selects*, and when you want to clean up the mess after your joyride, do a *drop*.

Documentation

In order to push our module into the *Documentation* application, we require a *Books.xml* and a *Docs.xml* file.

 Just like you should write tests while you are developing, you should write documentation while you are developing, not afterwards.

Example 4-21. [moduleroot]/etc/system/Books.xml

```xml
<?xml version="1.0" encoding="UTF-8"?>
<books>
  <book>
    <id>book:urn:org:netkernelbook:chapter4:mongodb</id>
    <title>MongoDB Database Tools</title>
    <desc>netkernelbook chapter4 mongodb database tools documentation</desc>
    <toc>
      <item
        id="urn:org:netkernelbook:chapter4:mongodb:guide"/>
      <item
        id="urn:org:netkernelbook:chapter4:mongodb:interfacereference"/>
    </toc>
  </book>
</books>
```

Example 4-22. [moduleroot]/etc/system/Docs.xml

```xml
<?xml version="1.0" encoding="UTF-8"?>
<docs>
  <doc>
    <id>urn:org:netkernelbook:chapter4:mongodb:guide</id>
    <title>Introduction to MongoDB</title>
    <desc>mongodb introduction</desc>
    <uri>res:/resources/documentation/doc_mongodb_introduction.txt</uri>
  </doc>
  <doc>
    <id>urn:org:netkernelbook:chapter4:mongodb:interfacereference</id>
    <title>Reference for MongoDB Interface</title>
    <desc>mongodb interface reference</desc>
    <uri>res:/resources/documentation/doc_mongodb_interface.txt</uri>
  </doc>
</docs>
```

So, we are going to have one book with two documents, a general introduction to MongoDB, and a reference to the MongoDB interface we developed. The funny thing is that the second document is practically going to write itself.

Example 4-23. [moduleroot]/resources/documentation/doc_mongodb_interface.txt

```
{endpoint}mongodb:interfaceEP{/endpoint}
```

One line—it's just one single line! Have a look at it: http://localhost:1060/books/?filter=mongodb. Is that cool or what? With very little effort during development, documentation is available and easy to maintain. Just one file remains to complete our documentation now.

Example 4-24. [moduleroot]/resources/documentation/doc_mongodb_introduction.txt

```
== Documentation Stub ==
This is a documentation stub.

For more information on editing documentation
see the [doc:sysadmin:guide:doc:editing|Editing Guide].
```

Yes, it's just a documentation stub. Don't you think I've blown the MongoDB trumpet hard enough already? You'll find all the information you need on the MongoDB website.

Interfacing

As you can see, it is not all that hard to bridge the gap between NetKernel and the following:

- Any third party code you want to try out
- Your company's current code
- Other possibilities

In my personal experience, I've approached this in two ways:

- Use the code as a NetKernel resource
- Use the data provided by the code as a NetKernel resource

The first option is preferred; the second is, however, an easier way to lower the resistance to change in your company.

Room for Improvement

There is major room for improvement here. Let's touch on one thing that would almost certainly be needed on the road toward the *real integration* (rather than just interfacing) of the MongoDB library. Take into account the *actions on the documents* in our database, and then we'll discuss *verbs* (that is, actions on resources).

SOURCE

Retrieve a representation of the identified resource.

SINK

Update the resource to reflect the information contained in the primary representation.

EXISTS

Test to see if a resource identifier can be resolved and the resource exists.

DELETE

Remove the resource from the space which currently contains it, and return the value TRUE if successful or FALSE if not successful.

NEW

Create a new resource and return an identifier for the created resource. If a primary representation is included in the request, use it to initialize the state of the resource.

Search http://localhost:1060/tools/search/ with the keyword *verbs*: the top hit contains all possible verbs, as well as the correct definition of a verb. Even without that information, you'll probably already agree that I didn't do ROC justice by using the default verb (SOURCE) for all my MongoDB requests. The above verbs and their definitions match the database actions perfectly.

So, if you feel like a challenge at this point, make a version 2.0.0 of the module that *does* do justice to ROC!

The download for this chapter can be found here (*http://dl.dropbox.com/u/65770556/ urn.org.netkernelbook.chapter4.mongodb-1.0.0.zip*).

## CHAPTER 5

Expanding Your Horizon

In this final chapter of the first part, we tie up a couple of loose ends. Afterward, you can (and should) strike out on your own. Come back to the chapters in the second part as and when you need them.

New Module Wizard

I made you work hard on the *[moduleroot]/module.xml* files so far. Even *First Module* had three rootspaces (the main one, one for tests, and one for documentation) that you had to type in from scratch.

Confession

Actually, we could have made *First Module* with hardly any work at all. <u>Point</u> *your browser* to *http://localhost:1060/tools/newmodule/* and fill out the forms. It is that easy. It registers your module with the NetKernel instance, too, and provides stubs for testing and documentation. The functionality it provides is the very same *First Module* provides.

This is no coincidence, by the way. I reverse-engineered (not a whole lot of work) a generated *First Module*, and that became my Chapter 1.

To Use or Not to Use

A generated stub module (for that is what it is) to start your development may work for you. It does not for me. While I do use my own simple templates to increase my productivity, absolute control over my sources is—for me—mandatory. So, I do not use a generated stub module and I do the registering myself.

Go with whatever makes you most productive. I'm old-school.

Exercise

Well, there's an obvious exercise here, is there not? See how quickly you can make a *Second Module*. This should not take you more than five minutes!

Visualizer

You will come to love this tool. In fact, you are going to be angry that I did not introduce it earlier, for you had problems with the previous chapters, did you not? Of course you did. A small typo here and there and things didn't work as the book said they would. You had to go back and check, a painstaking process.

The *Visualizer* is reachable through the *Backend HTTPFulcrum Control Panel* in the *Developer* panel, to be exact. Or you can <u>point</u> *your browser* at *http://localhost:1060/ tools/ae/view/visualizer*.

 Because detail is very important in this section, the screenshots have not been cropped or otherwise manipulated. As a consequence, most had to be rotated to fit. Forgive me for any inconvenience that may cause.

We are going to make use of our *First Module* to discuss the use of the Visualizer.

1. You should be looking at the Visualizer (Figure 5-1).

2. <u>Enter</u> the following *regular expression* in the input field that has *Root request regex filter* inside.

        .*/firstmodule/helloservice.*

3. <u>Select</u> the *Start button.*

4. <u>Point</u> *your browser* at the following (one after the other, order does not matter) URLs:

        http://localhost:8080/firstmodule/helloservice
        http://localhost:8080/firstmodule/helloservice/
        http://localhost:8080/firstmodule/helloservice/tom

5. <u>Point</u> *your browser* at the Visualizer again:

        http://localhost:1060/tools/ae/view/visualizer

6. <u>Select</u> the *Stop button* (Figure 5-2).

Right, what did we accomplish here? The Visualizer allows you to capture complete trace information about *root requests* processed by NetKernel. It is normally off, so you have to start it first. The regular expression limits the root requests that are traced.

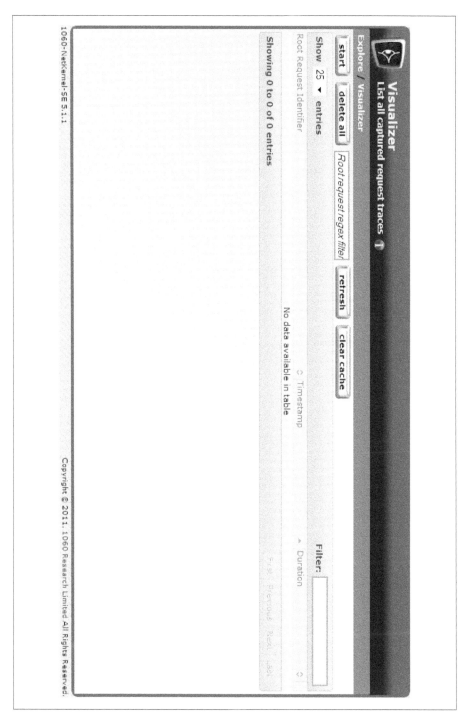

Figure 5-1. Visualizer

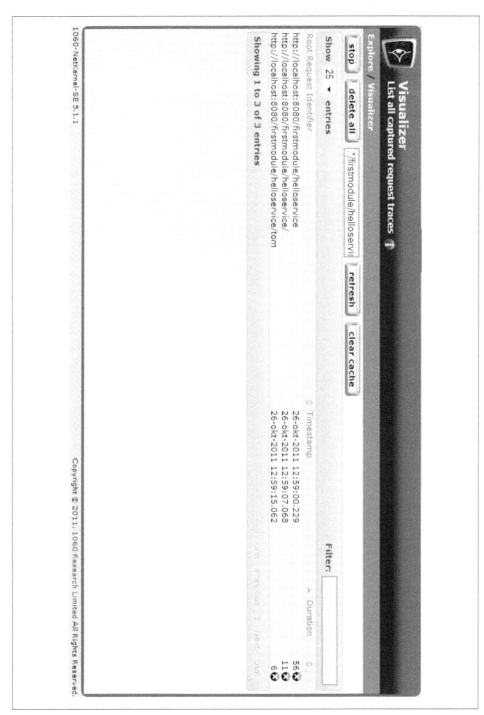

Figure 5-2. Visualizer First Module

The above begs the question, what is a *root request*? It is an external event/request injected into NetKernel through a transport. This in turn is explained best by its most common case: a request to the *Frontend HTTPFulcrum*. And you just did three of those.

As you know by now, a root request usually initiates subrequests and those subrequests initiate further sub-requests down to arbitrary depths into your application. The capturing isn't just surface deep. It is a tree, and you'll have access to all of it.

 Capturing visualizer traces has *close to zero* performance overhead to an executing system! Due to the immutability of resource representations, capturing simply involves hanging on to resource representations for longer than otherwise would be needed. So, the only penalty is memory.

What you can see in Figure 5-3 is what you get when you <u>select</u> the *http://localhost: 8080/helloservice* root request capture in the Visualizer and then <u>pick</u> *View Request Trace* from the list.

Yes, I do know that particular request results in a *Request Resolution Failure*. The visualizer does not care; a request was injected into NetKernel, and the Visualizer captures the complete tree of what happened next.

If you <u>select</u> the *[none]* on the third line under the *Physical Endpoint/Callstack* header and then <u>pick</u> *View Request Details* from the list, you can see (Figure 5-4) what happened next, too.

It looks remarkably like the Request Resolution trace tool that we used in Chapter 4, does it not? What it tells us is that there's no match for our request. The remainder of the tree shows how the exception is turned into a response.

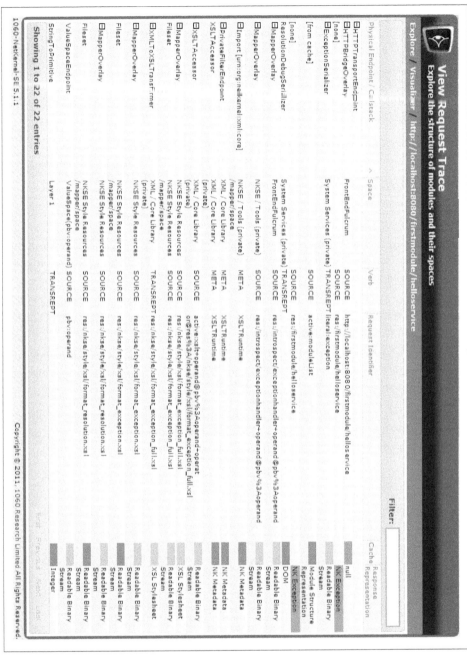

Figure 5-3. View Request Trace—Exception

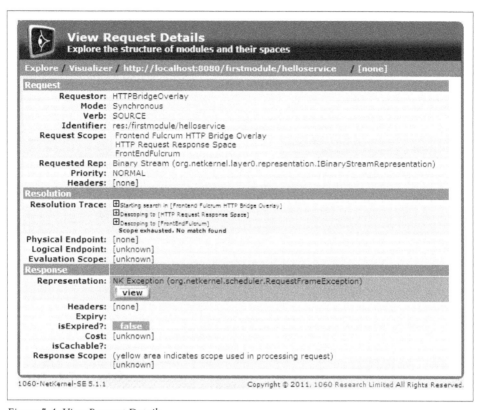

Figure 5-4. View Request Details

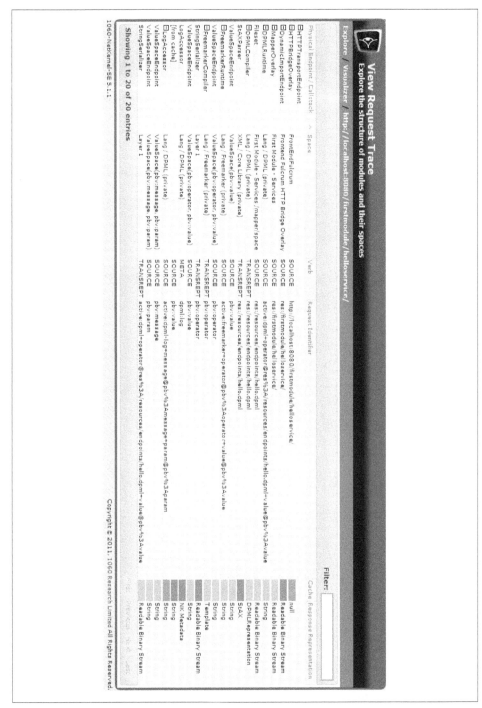

Figure 5-5. View Request Trace—Resolved

There's a bit more to see (Figure 5-5) when you <u>select</u> the *http://localhost:8080/hello-service/* root request capture in the Visualizer and then <u>pick</u> *View Request Trace* from the list, obviously, since this request did resolve.

Run through the tree, and notice how you can see every actual subrequest. You can see where it comes from, how it resolves and what its response is. In fact, this is what you can see:

1. The invoked endpoint
2. The address space, which hosts the endpoint
3. The request verb
4. The request identifier
5. Cache status of the response
6. Representation of the response

Remember that I said—way back—that everything is a resource, including your code? <u>Select</u> the *Fileset* physical endpoint and then <u>pick</u> *View Response* from the list. Recognize the DPML code?

I cannot give you the actual link. Remember that everything you see in the Visualizer is a resource representation kept in a cache a bit longer than usual. Where it is in the cache (and hence the link) depends on your NetKernel instance. My link would not work for you.

If NetKernel provided a way to represent compiled DPML in a browser, you'd be able to see that in the next line. It doesn't, but you can see the object there, and a representation could be developed.

I'm leaving the third root request capture as an exercise for you. The differences between it and the second one are minimal. Can you find them, and can you see how this tool can help you immensely during development as well as during debugging?

I've kept quiet about something, but by now you're probably wondering why your traces don't look anything like mine, aren't you? In fact, they will probably look more like Figure 5-6. Also, note the duration difference.

The reason is *caching*. NetKernel has a truly superior caching mechanism, and if you've been experimenting with *First Module* for a bit, most—if not all—of its sub-requests will be cached.

This is something to keep in mind when you are troubleshooting. If you want to make sure caching is not in effect, make sure to <u>select</u> *clear cache* before starting your trace!

This is what I did to create the examples above. Forgive me for cheating.

Apposite

Not being a native English speaker or writer, I had to look up the meaning of *Apposite*. And I must say, it is an apposite term.

SE Versus EE

The *NetKernel Standard Edition* is a complete environment (if this book is not proof of that, I don't know what is). In a minute, we'll see how you can add some *extra batteries* to that environment.

So, what does the *NetKernel Enterprise Edition* add to that? Mainly the tools (extra modules) you need to manage a big environment, performance-wise, security-wise, and deployment-wise.

 While I am not in any way affiliated with 1060 Research, I'm going to take a moment to promote buying a license for *NetKernel Enterprise Edition*. It's worth it! Compare the price to the price your company pays for the application server of [enter big company name here] for a single core (!) and you'll laugh. Compare the power it delivers to the same . . . and you'll laugh harder still, though you'll be somewhat green (or *blue* perhaps?) when you realize the amounts you've been throwing out of the window.

If you're in a small outfit (or have to work yourself through a lot of resistance),[1] consider getting a support license. Most companies only promise, and these guys deliver. Fair is fair.

So far, we've used Apposite only in Appendix A to update packages after the initial install. For SE, that is the main use of Apposite. In EE, there's the ARP tool, *Apposite Repository Publisher*, which allows you to manage and create (and secure) your own (company) repositories, an indispensable tool for any environment that has (more than) a couple of instances!

You can find a video tutorial (this requires access to the Internet) of the ARP tool in the SE Tutorial Guide at *http://localhost:1060/book/view/book:tutorial:guide/*. And yes, I read the *"Open source projects can get a free copy of ARP on request"* line, too. If you

---

1. Been there, done that.

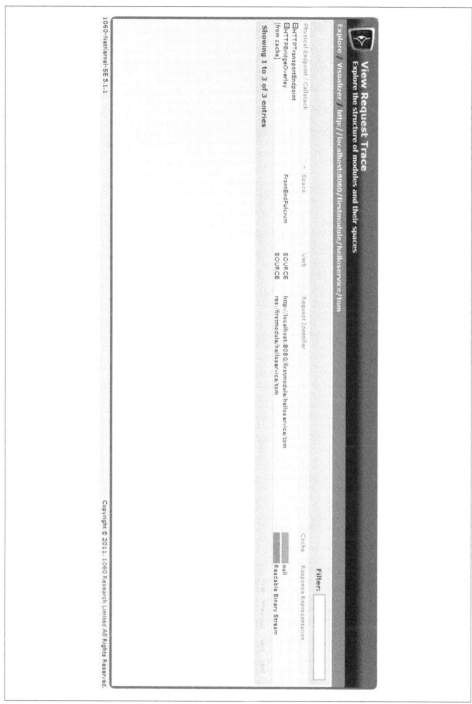

Figure 5-6. Cache effect

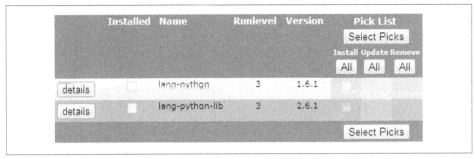

Figure 5-7. Filters applied

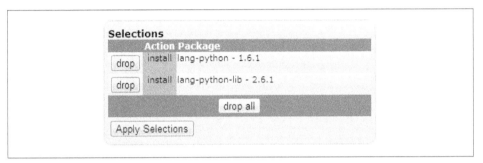

Figure 5-8. Selections

qualify, by all means request it. If you don't, this is the kind of tool that *on its own* justifies a EE license.

Extra Batteries

At last, I get to force Python upon you . . . I mean, I'll use Python to show how to add functionality (i.e., another language to develop with) to your NetKernel instance.

What I want you to do is this:

1. <u>Point</u> *your browser at* http://localhost:1060/tools/apposite/.
2. <u>Enter</u> *python in the* "Name Matches" *field*.
3. <u>Select</u> *Apply Filters* (Figure 5-7).

Next, you :

1. <u>Tick</u> *both modules in the Install* column.
2. <u>Select</u> *Select Picks* (Figure 5-8).

<u>Select</u> *Apply Selections*.

<u>Select</u> *Refresh* (Figure 5-9).

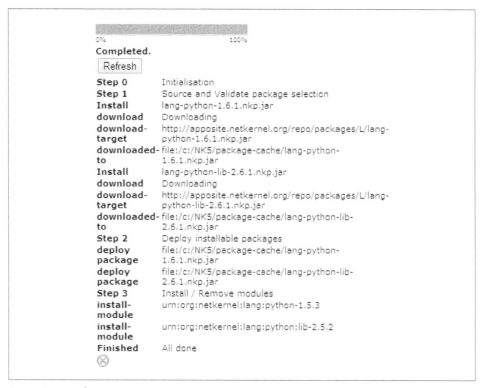

Figure 5-9. Deployment

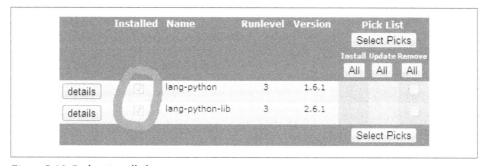

Figure 5-10. Python installed

You now have the Python language at your disposal (Figure 5-10).

Updating your packages to the latest version on the official repository is covered in Appendix A, and getting a local copy of that official repository and repointing your instance to that copy is covered in Appendix B. You can add different repositories to get packages from, but rolling your own repository is reserved for *Enterprise Edition* users.

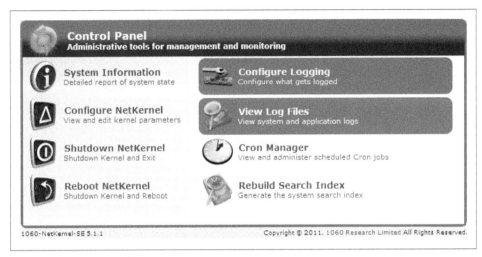

Figure 5-11. Logging tools

Packaging

You might expect me to discuss http://localhost:1060/tools/packager/ here. By all means, check it out, and for *Standard Edition*, it is overkill in my opinion. If you want to distribute a module, zip the *[moduleroot]* directory. True, if you unpack it in another instance, you'll have to modify *[install]/etc/modules.xml* manually, but that's not too hard to remember, is it?

Logging

You can read my thoughts on *logging* in the first section of Chapter 4. However, it's not because logging is often used incorrectly that it isn't necessary. NetKernel has a good logging system *on board*.

The stuff below is about using that existing logging system in NetKernel (plugging in your own application), not about rolling your own. That topic would merit a(nother) book of its own.

Tools

Through the *Backend HTTPFulcrum—Control Panel*, you can reach the two tools of the logging system (Figure 5-11).

 The above image is f two screenshots superimposed. You cannot normally select two options at the same time.

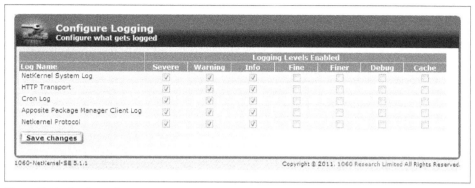

Figure 5-12. Configure logging

With *Configure Logging*, you can modify the granularity of the *existing logs* (Figure 5-12).

View Log Files is a simple, but most of the time sufficient, viewer for the *existing logs* (Figure 5-13).

Surely you noticed me emphasizing *existing logs* twice or thrice now. So, what about creating a new application log? How does one go about that? Well, it is a bit counterintuitive.

Plugging In

The counterintuitive part about it is that a new application log comes into existence by using it. That's right, there's no *Application Log Creation* tool and not a *dynamic import* either.

I expected a dynamic import, but think about it: you control when and where you want to use a certain log. You therefore don't need to create it beforehand (maybe you'll never use it), and logging only needs a way out of your module, not a way in.

You are already plugged in

Yes, you are! Our *First Module* has logging. Why don't you <u>try</u> the following *URLs* again:

```
http://localhost:8080/firstmodule/helloservice/
http://localhost:8080/firstmodule/helloservice/tom
```

Now, <u>navigate</u> to the *logviewer*, and <u>select</u> the *NetKernel System Log*. You may have to <u>select</u> the *update button* too, but then you should see the loggings (your datetime stamps will differ, of course) in Figure 5-14.

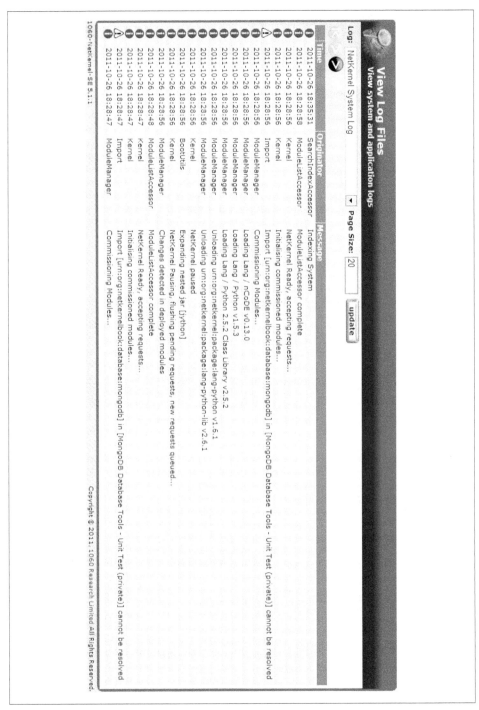

Figure 5-13. View log files

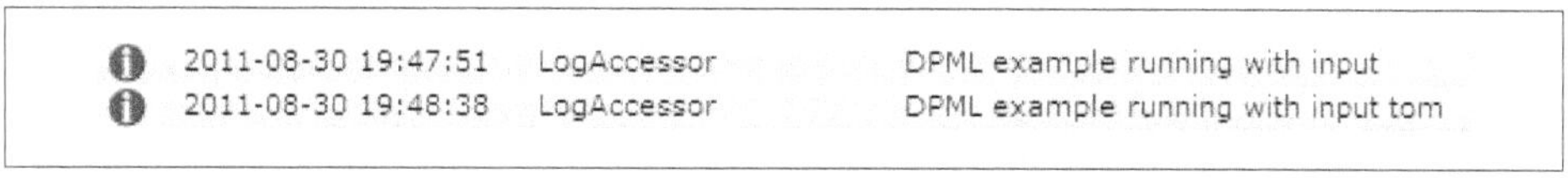

	2011-08-30 19:47:51	LogAccessor	DPML example running with input
	2011-08-30 19:48:38	LogAccessor	DPML example running with input tom

Figure 5-14. NetKernel System Log

Have another look at the *hello.dpml* code in Chapter 1 to see how we accomplished this. Logging in DPML automatically goes to the default log and unless you specify one of your own (which we'll do in a minute), that is the NetKernel System Log.

LogConfig

Your application's default log configuration goes into *[moduleroot]/etc/system/LogConfig.xml*.

If you don't provide one there, NetKernel will search any accessible spaces until it finds one. If it doesn't, the configuration of the NetKernel System Log, which is in *[install]/etc/KernelLogConfig.xml* is used. This also explains why the logging in *First Module* works.

```
<log>
    <id>NetKernel</id>
    <name>NetKernel System Log</name>
    <handlers>
        <handler>
            <instance>
                <class>org.netkernel.layer0.logging.LogFileHandler</class>
                <string>%b/log/netkernel-%g.log</string>
                <int>50000000</int>
                <int>3</int>
                <boolean>true</boolean>
            </instance>
            <formatterClass>org.netkernel.layer0.logging.XMLFormatter</formatterClass>
        </handler>
        <handler>
            <instance>
                <class>java.util.logging.ConsoleHandler</class>
            </instance>
            <formatterClass>org.netkernel.layer0.logging.ConsoleFormatter</
formatterClass>
        </handler>
    </handlers>
</log>
```

The configuration is very straightforward. A log has one or more *handlers* each handler has an *instance* that processes the loggings, and a *formatter*, which QED-formats the loggings.

As you can see, the NetKernel System Log has two handlers, which means each logging gets processed twice (it is sent to both file and console). While this makes sense for a system log, it does not for your average application log. One handler will do fine.

So, once more we turn back to *First Module* and create a *[moduleroot]/etc/LogConfig.xml* for it.

```
<log>
  <id>HelloServiceLog</id>
  <name>Hello Service Log</name>
  <handlers>
    <handler>
      <instance>
        <class>org.netkernel.layer0.logging.LogFileHandler</class>
        <string>%b/log/helloservice-%g.log</string>
        <int>50000000</int>
        <int>3</int>
        <boolean>true</boolean>
      </instance>
      <formatterClass>org.netkernel.layer0.logging.XMLFormatter</formatterClass>
    </handler>
  </handlers>
</log>
```

As I said before, this section is about using the existing log system, so I'm using the existing classes *LogFileHandler* and *XMLFormatter*. These are slightly extended versions of *java.util.logging.FileHandler* and *java.util.logging.XMLFormatter*. Nothing fancy.

The arguments passed to the *LogFileHandler* are:

1. A pattern that identifies the file used for logging. *%b* stands for *base* and equals [install]. *%g* stands for *generation*, starts at 0, and increases with each file rotation (see next argument).

2. The size (in bytes) the logfile can grow to before a next generation is started (a logrotate, in other words).

3. The number of generations the logfile can have before the oldest—0—generation is overwritten.

4. A boolean indicating if the logfile can be appended to (true) or not (false).

Well, we now have a logging configuration for *First Module*, and the endpoint itself already does the actual logging. All that's left is to link the two together. In order to do that, you need to alter the *space definition* for our endpoint in *[moduleroot]/module.xml* a bit.

```
<space>
  <fileset>
    <regex>res:/resources/endpoints/.*</regex>
  </fileset>
```

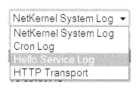

Figure 5-15. Log Selection

```
<fileset>
  <regex>res:/etc/system/LogConfig.xml</regex>
</fileset>
<import>
  <uri>urn:org:netkernel:lang:dpml</uri>
</import>
<import>
  <uri>urn:org:netkernel:lang:freemarker</uri>
</import>
</space>
```

Allow NetKernel to register this change to the module. Then <u>try</u> the following URLs again:

```
http://localhost:8080/firstmodule/helloservice/
http://localhost:8080/firstmodule/helloservice/tom
```

Now, <u>navigate</u> to the *logviewer*, and you should have one more log to select (Figure 5-15).

Non DPML

While DPML is a very powerful language (there is a whole chapter devoted to it in Part II), most people will want to use their own favorite language, and that is just fine. All you have to do is consider the context.

In Chapter 4, I briefly discussed the *context* object, which is always there for all non-DPML languages in NetKernel. This object delivers (and gives you access to) exactly what it says: the *context* in which your request is executed. As it happens, it also implements the *org.netkernel.layer0.nkf.INKFLocale* interface, which provides it with logging methods:

- logFormatted—default log
- logFormatted—specific log
- logRaw—default log
- logRaw—specific log

Now, this is where it pays off to have NetKernel instances (definitely your development instances) run on a JDK instead of on a JRE, because you are going to want to see the *javadocs* for INKFLocale as well as for NKFContextImpl (the context class). In order to generate *javadocs*, you need a JDK.

The methods are very straightforward:

```
context.logRaw(context.LEVEL_DEBUG,'My message');
context.logRaw('etc/system/LogConfig.xml',context.LEVEL_INFO,'Your message');
context.logRaw(LogManager.DEFAULT_LOG,context.LEVEL_WARNING,'His message');
context.logRaw('etc/system/AnotherLogConfig.xml',context.LEVEL_SEVERE,'Her message');
```

If you can see that the first three loggings use the same configuration (and thus will be logged to the same log), you've grasped the logging system. Where the last logging goes depends on what is in *[moduleroot]/etc/system/AnotherLogConfig.xml*. Note that the last logging would be impossible in DPML.

Message Bundles

If you've been paying attention to this logging section, you may have remarked on at least two things:

1. The DPML logging used percent substitutions, which I didn't reproduce in the context examples.
2. I provided no examples for the *logFormatted* methods.

The first point is covered by yet another method (did I say you need those *javadocs* already?) from INKFLocale, *formatRaw*.

For the second point, I need to introduce *message bundles*. Message bundles are implemented through a *[moduleroot]/etc/message.properties* file.

```
DB_SUCCESS=sucessful [%1] for [%2] key [%3]
DB_FAILURE=failed [%1] for [%2] key [%3]
```

Next, make sure *res:/etc/message.properties* is in scope, and then the examples can look like this:

```
context.logFormatted(context.LEVEL_DEBUG, 'DB_SUCCESS', 'insert',
'entityname' ,entity_id);
context.logFormatted('etc/system/LogConfig.xml', context.LEVEL_INFO, 'DB_FAILURE',
'update', 'entityname', entity_id);
context.logFormatted(LogManager.DEFAULT_LOG, context.LEVEL_WARNING, 'DB_FAILURE',
'delete', 'entityname', entity_id);
context.logFormatted('etc/system/AnotherLogConfig.xml', context.LEVEL_SEVERE,
'DB_FAILURE', 'select', 'entityname', entity_id);
```

Viewlog Accessor

You may not like the viewer in the Backend HTTPFulcrum, or you do, but you want a more fine-grained control on who can see what.

Now, you can always completely write your own viewer, of course, but when you've used the *LogFileHandler—XMLFormatter* combination in your configuration, you can also make use of the accessor used in the Backend HTTPFulcrum viewer. For example:

```
netkernel:/log/HelloServiceLog/0/10
```

So, the accessor requires the id of the log, an offset (starting point back from the end of the log file), and a count (number of loggings to retrieve at most).

 Do you hear or read the words *easy paging* for your viewer in the above? I do!

Check out *http://localhost:1060/book/view/book:ext:system:book/doc:ext:system:log* for more information (especially for the *Import Requirements*).

Conclusion

Logging is available in NetKernel. Use it, don't abuse it!

## PART II

Batteries Included

I once bought my kids a set of batteries for Christmas with a note on it saying, toys not included . . . —Bernard Manning

## CHAPTER 6

DPML

Declarative-Request Process Markup Language (DPML) is a heavyweight name for a simple, lightweight language. It has a simple syntax to do one thing extremely well, resource request handling.

Glue

You're probably wondering why you should learn yet another language, and one with a limited use, too. The chance you heard of DPML before you started with NetKernel is zero.

Remember the *hello.dpml* program from *FirstModule*?

```
<?xml version="1.0" encoding="UTF-8"?>
<sequence>
  <request assignment="response">
    <identifier>active:freemarker</identifier>
    <argument name="operator">
      <literal type="string">Input value: ${value}</literal>
    </argument>
    <argument name="value">arg:value</argument>
  </request>
  <log>
    <message>
     <literal type="string">DPML example running with input %1</literal>
    </message>
    <param>arg:value</param>
  </log>
</sequence>
```

The **hello.groovy** equivalent looks like this:

```
import org.netkernel.layer0.nkf.NKFException;
import org.netkernel.layer0.nkf.INKFRequestReadOnly;

value = context.source("arg:value", String.class);

subrequest_url = "active:freemarker";
```

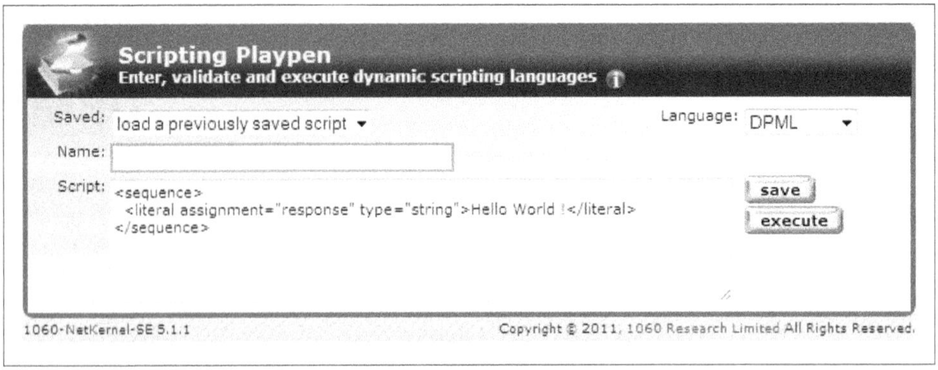

Figure 6-1. DPML Hello World

```
subrequest    = context.createRequest(subrequest_url);
subrequest.setVerb(INKFRequestReadOnly.VERB_SOURCE);
subrequest.addArgumentByValue("operator",'Input value: ${value}');
subrequest.addArgumentByValue("value",value);
subrequest.setRepresentationClass(String.class);
resultString  = context.issueRequest(subrequest);

logString = context.formatRaw('DPML example running with input %1',value);
context.logRaw(context.LEVEL_INFO,logString);

response  = context.createResponseFrom(resultString);
response.setMimeType('text/plain');
response.setExpiry(response.EXPIRY_ALWAYS);
```

The actual number of lines does not differ all that much, but you'll agree with me that you need to know a lot more of the NetKernel Foundation API (NKF API) to write the Groovy program.

True, you'll say, but after one masters the NKF API for one's favorite language, what is gained by learning DPML then?

Well, while I write my services and tools in Python (or Groovy or Java), the gluing-it-all-together (composition) is more often than not done with DPML. Why? Because it is the language that best fits that job. [1]

Building Blocks

I am going to approach this the way most programming language books approach it. The first thing they usually do is show a "Hello World" program.

Now, walking you through the creation of a module to experiment with DPML should be unnecessary at this stage. For the examples in this chapter, I'm going to use the *Scripting Playpen*. <u>Point</u> your *browser* at *http://localhost:1060/tools/scriptplaypen*.

---

1. Give me the tools, and I'll finish the job!

Figure 6-1 takes care of all the preliminaries. We'll discuss the script in detail in a minute. Select *execute* if you want to see it in action.

Basics

From the documentation, you can learn that DPML is an XML representation of an AST, an *Abstract Syntax Tree*. I don't know about you, but I had to look up the meaning of AST.

So, are there benefits to the fact that DPML *transrepts* to an AST rather than directly to Java or elsewhere. Well, I can think of two:

1. Using another format, other than XML, that is, for DPML should be easy.
2. Using another implementation language, other than Java, that is, for DPML should be easy.

The latter is not completely true since the AST is rather Java specific (there is abstract and abstract, apparently), but all in all, DPML is a very interesting example of how to develop a new language.

The most important basic fact to know about DPML, however, is this: you cannot *do* anything with DPML!

I'm not kidding. Take simple arithmetic. 1 + 1 = ? You can do this in any programming language, but you can't do this in DPML.

DPML handles requests and request responses. The first *1* is a resource that can be obtained through a request or that is literal. So is the second *1*. So are the + and the =. All these can be passed to another request, for example, to an *active:calculate* (provided by the *urn.org.netkernel.lang.math module*). The response can be passed to yet another request or may be the final response of the DPML program itself, but DPML *can not itself act* upon the response.

Did that fact take hold in your brain ? Then you are ready to dive into DPML.

Sequence

A *sequence* executes statements in order of appearance. It can be the root element of a DPML program.

```
<sequence>
  <literal assignment="response" type="string">Hello World!</literal>
</sequence>
```

Literal

The *literal* statement is a *special request statement* that has the specified value as its response. It cannot be the root element of a DPML program.

Figure 6-2. Sequence result

Through the *assignment* attribute. the response of a request can be given a label so you can refer to it again (as *this:label*). The final response of the DPML program should be labeled *response*. For example:

```
<sequence>
  <literal assignment="afternoon" type="string">Good Afternoon</literal>
  <literal assignment="response" type="string">Good Evening</literal>
  <literal assignment="goodbye" type="string">Goodbye</literal>
</sequence>
```

You can see the result in Figure 6-2.

The third *literal* statement is correct and gets executed, just like the other two. But it is the response of the second statement that is labelled *response* and thus gets returned.

Request

If there are special request statements there have to be *normal request statements*, too. And these are no doubt familiar as they are exactly what you'd find in a *module.xml*. A request statement cannot be the root element of a DPML program.

```
<sequence>
  <request assignment="response">
    <identifier>active:freemarker</identifier>
    <argument name="operator">
      <literal type="string">${value?upper_case}</literal>
    </argument>
    <argument name="value">
      <literal type="string">Banana</literal>
    </argument>
  </request>
</sequence>
```

You can see the result in Figure 6-3.

Figure 6-3. Request result

I am going to use the above program to press home the point again: you can't *do* anything with DPML! It does not do math, it does not have string functions.

It can however handle a request that does the job. I could have done it with *XSLT*, a custom-made *active:toUpper* or whatever, I chose *Freemarker*.

Conditional Processing

DPML does not provide the classic *if-then-else* structure. No, it doesn't. Let me say it one final time: you can't *do* anything with DPML! It doesn't have if-then-else.

It can, however, handle a request that does the job. And an *active:if* tool is available. You can use this tool in any of the other scripting languages as well, although those do usually have an if-then-else of their own.

```
<sequence>
  <request assignment="response">
    <identifier>meta:dpml:if</identifier>
    <argument name="cond">
      <request>
        <identifier>active:freemarker</identifier>
        <argument name="operator">
          <literal type="string">${value?contains("Ban")?string}</literal>
        </argument>
        <argument name="value">
          <literal type="string">Banana</literal>
        </argument>
      </request>
    </argument>
    <argument name="then">
      <literal type="string">Banana contains Ban</literal>
    </argument>
    <argument name="else">
      <literal type="string">Banana does not contain ban</literal>
    </argument>
```

```
    </request>
  </sequence>
```

That covers the then branch. If you want to make sure the else branch works, too, change the operator argument to this:

```
<literal type="string">${value?contains("ban")?string}</literal>
```

 Using the *meta:* scheme to call the logical endpoint identifier sets up a request according to the grammar of the endpoint. You need no knowledge of the type of grammar or how it was built. Just add the arguments, and you are set.

DPML does not provide the classic *switch* (or case, or whatever your favorite language calls it) structure.

It can, however—you guessed it—handle a request that does the job, and an *active:switch* tool is available.

```
<sequence>
  <request assignment="response">
    <identifier>meta:dpml:switch</identifier>
    <argument name="cond">
      <request>
        <identifier>active:freemarker</identifier>
        <argument name="operator">
          <literal type="string">${value?contains("ban")?string}</literal>
        </argument>
        <argument name="value">
          <literal type="string">Banana</literal>
        </argument>
      </request>
    </argument>
    <argument name="then">
      <literal type="string">Banana contains Ban</literal>
    </argument>
    <argument name="cond">
      <request>
        <identifier>active:freemarker</identifier>
        <argument name="operator">
          <literal type="string">${value?contains("app")?string}</literal>
        </argument>
        <argument name="value">
          <literal type="string">Apple</literal>
        </argument>
      </request>
    </argument>
    <argument name="then">
      <literal type="string">Apple contains App</literal>
    </argument>
    <argument name="otherwise">
      <literal type="string">Something completely different</literal>
    </argument>
```

```
    </request>
  </sequence>
```

You can no doubt figure out how to test all branches yourself by now.

Iterative Processing

DPML does not provide the classic *for-loop* structure.

It can, however, handle a request that does the job, and an *active:ncodeForEach* tool is available. The tool implements the *iterator-based for-loop* (*http://en.wikipedia.org/wiki/Foreach*) which is a generalization of the common numeric range type of for-loop (*http://en.wikipedia.org/wiki/For_loop*) as it allows for the enumeration of sets of items other than number sequences.

nCoDE gets a chapter of its own further on in the book. For now, think of it as *Visual DPML*.

```
<sequence>
  <request assignment="result">
    <identifier>meta:ncode:builtin:foreach</identifier>
    <argument name="collection">
      <request>
        <identifier>active:groovy</identifier>
        <argument name="operator">
          <literal type="string">
            context.createResponseFrom(0..4);
          </literal>
        </argument>
      </request>
    </argument>
    <argument name="do">
      <request>
        <identifier>active:groovy</identifier>
        <argument name="operator">
          <literal type="string">
            message=context.source("arg:item");
            context.createResponseFrom(message.toString());
          </literal>
        </argument>
        <argument name="item">foreach:item</argument>
      </request>
    </argument>
  </request>
  <request assignment="response">
    <identifier>meta:ncode:builtin:tostring</identifier>
    <argument name="operand">this:result</argument>
  </request>
</sequence>
```

That looks complicated for a for-loop. Here's the pseudocode for what goes on :

```
for each item in collection:
    do something to item
```

The *collection* attribute has to be a *java.lang.Iterable*. DPML does not (this is getting boring, is it not?) provide that, but it can handle a request that does the job. In this case, that's a small inline Groovy program that returns an *iterable* range of numbers. It could have been an array of strings, of XML documents, and so on.

DPML does requests, so the *do* attribute is a request. It's nothing fancy; note that the *active:ncodeForEach* tool provides three extra arguments that can be passed to that request:

foreach:item
> The current item.

foreach:index
> The index of the current item.

foreach:count
> The total number of lines.

That is your basic DPML for-loop. So, why is there a second request in the sequence? Actually, there does not have to be one. I could have assigned the *active:ncodeForEach* request directly to the response. However, it returns a *java.lang.Iterable* containing the responses of each iteration. There is no transreptor available for a *java.lang.Iterable*, so it can not be shown in your browser (well, the transreptor error is shown). Since this is somewhat silly for an example, I've used the *active:ncodeToString* tool to provide the simplest transreption available for any Java object: turn it into a string.

Next to the mandatory *collection* and *do* arguments, *active:ncodeForEach* has two optional arguments that can make things a lot more interesting:

async
> When set to 0 or greater, iterations (do's) will be launched asynchronously, the number indicating the timeout in milliseconds.

tolerant
> When set to true, failed iterations (do's) will be ignored and return null.

The combination of *async set to 0* and *tolerant set to true* is also known as the *fire-and-forget* pattern.

DPML does not provide the classic *while-loop* structure.

It can, however, handle a request that does the job, and an *active:ncodeWhile* tool is available.

```
<sequence>
  <request assignment="result">
    <identifier>meta:ncode:builtin:while</identifier>
```

```
<argument name="condition">
  <request>
    <identifier>active:groovy</identifier>
    <argument name="operator">
      <literal type="string">
        import org.netkernel.layer0.nkf.INKFResponse;
        random = new Random()
        randomInt = random.nextInt()
        if ((randomInt%2)){
         response = context.createResponseFrom(true);
        }
        else {
          response = context.createResponseFrom(false);
        }
        response.setExpiry(INKFResponse.EXPIRY_ALWAYS);
      </literal>
    </argument>
  </request>
</argument>
<argument name="do">
  <request>
    <identifier>active:groovy</identifier>
    <argument name="operator">
      <literal type="string">
        message="hit";
        context.createResponseFrom(message.toString());
      </literal>
    </argument>
  </request>
</argument>
</request>
<request assignment="response">
  <identifier>meta:ncode:builtin:tostring</identifier>
  <argument name="operand">this:result</argument>
</request>
</sequence>
```

DPML does not provide the classic *until-loop* structure.

It can, however, handle a request that does the job, and an *active:ncodeUntil* tool is available.

```
<sequence>
  <request assignment="result">
    <identifier>meta:ncode:builtin:until</identifier>
    <argument name="do">
      <request>
        <identifier>active:groovy</identifier>
        <argument name="operator">
          <literal type="string">
            message="hit";
            context.createResponseFrom(message.toString());
          </literal>
        </argument>
      </request>
    </argument>
```

```
    <argument name="condition">
      <request>
        <identifier>active:groovy</identifier>
        <argument name="operator">
          <literal type="string">
            import org.netkernel.layer0.nkf.INKFResponse;
            random = new Random()
            randomInt = random.nextInt()
            if ((randomInt%2)){
             response = context.createResponseFrom(true);
            }
            else {
              response = context.createResponseFrom(false);
            }
            response.setExpiry(INKFResponse.EXPIRY_ALWAYS);
          </literal>
        </argument>
      </request>
    </argument>
  </request>
  <request assignment="response">
    <identifier>meta:ncode:builtin:tostring</identifier>
    <argument name="operand">this:result</argument>
  </request>
</sequence>
```

You can see the result in Figure 6-4.

Figure 6-4. While result

Exception Handling

DPML does not provide a *try-catch-finally* structure.

It can, however, handle a request that does the job, and an *active:exception* tool is available.

```
<sequence>
  <request assignment="response">
    <identifier>meta:dpml:exception</identifier>
    <argument name="try">
      <request>
```

```
      <identifier>active:groovy</identifier>
      <argument name="operator">
        <literal type="string">
          context.createResponseFrom(1/0);
        </literal>
      </argument>
    </request>
  </argument>
  <argument name="catch">
    <request>
      <identifier>active:groovy</identifier>
      <argument name="operator">
        <literal type="string">
          message = context.source("arg:message");
          context.createResponseFrom(message);
        </literal>
      </argument>
      <argument name="message">exception:message</argument>
    </request>
  </argument>
  </request>
</sequence>
```

The request for the *catch-attribute* has access to the exception through the following extra attributes:

exception:raw
: the complete exception

exception:id
: the exception id

exception:message
: the exception message

If you provide a *finally-attribute*, the request you specify inside is executed regardless of whether the *try* or the *catch* prevails. The response of the request is ignored.

```
<sequence>
  <request assignment="response">
    <identifier>meta:dpml:exception</identifier>
    <argument name="try">
      <request>
        <identifier>active:groovy</identifier>
        <argument name="operator">
          <literal type="string">
            context.createResponseFrom(1/0);
          </literal>
        </argument>
      </request>
    </argument>
    <argument name="catch">
      <request>
        <identifier>active:groovy</identifier>
        <argument name="operator">
          <literal type="string">
```

```
            message = context.source("arg:message");
            context.createResponseFrom(message);
          </literal>
        </argument>
        <argument name="message">exception:message</argument>
      </request>
    </argument>
    <argument name="finally">
      <request>
        <identifier>active:groovy</identifier>
        <argument name="operator">
          <literal type="string">
            println "I'm executed whatever happens but my response is ignored."
          </literal>
        </argument>
      </request>
    </argument>
  </request>
</sequence>
```

DPML does not provide a way to *throw* your own exceptions.

It can, however, handle a request that does the job, and an *active:throw* tool is available.

```
<sequence>
  <request assignment="response">
    <identifier>meta:dpml:throw</identifier>
    <argument name="id">
      <literal type="string">Something Went Wrong Error</literal>
    </argument>
  </request>
</sequence>
```

You can use *active:throw* to insert information in an existing exception. The following example uses the two optional attributes, *message* and *cause*, to do so.

```
<sequence>
  <request assignment="response">
    <identifier>meta:dpml:exception</identifier>
    <argument name="try">
      <request>
        <identifier>active:groovy</identifier>
        <argument name="operator">
          <literal type="string">
            context.createResponseFrom(1/0);
          </literal>
        </argument>
      </request>
    </argument>
    <argument name="catch">
      <request assignment="response">
        <identifier>meta:dpml:throw</identifier>
        <argument name="id">
          <literal type="string">Something Went Wrong Error</literal>
        </argument>
        <argument name="message">
```

```
        <request>
          <identifier>active:groovy</identifier>
          <argument name="operator">
            <literal type="string">
              context.createResponseFrom("You can't 1 divide by 0");
            </literal>
          </argument>
        </request>
      </argument>
      <argument name="cause">exception:raw</argument>
    </request>
  </argument>
  </request>
</sequence>
```

You can see in Figure 6-5 what information is inserted into the exception trace.

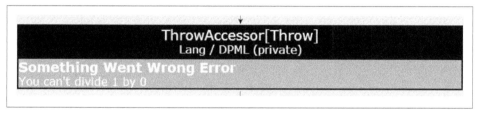

Figure 6-5. Exception

Making Life Easier

As stated earlier, DPML *cannot itself act* upon the request response(s)

However, an *active:modify-response* tool is provided. It can't touch the resource representation of the response (those are immutable, remember?), but it can change the headers. You'll use this tool mainly on the final response.

```
<sequence>
  <request assignment="response">
    <identifier>active:groovy</identifier>
    <argument name="operator">
      <literal type="string">
        import org.netkernel.layer0.nkf.INKFResponse;

        myUUID   = UUID.randomUUID().toString();
        response = context.createResponseFrom(myUUID);

        response.setExpiry(INKFResponse.EXPIRY_ALWAYS);
      </literal>
    </argument>
  </request>
  <request assignment="response">
    <identifier>meta:dpml:modify-response</identifier>
    <argument name="operand">this:response</argument>
    <argument name="config">
      <literal type="xml">
```

```
        <config>
          <header name="mime">text/plain</header>
          <expiry method="CONSTANT">5000</expiry>
        </config>
      </literal>
    </argument>
  </request>
</sequence>
```

Since the above program was a bit of a stumbling block for me, I'm going to explain it in a bit more detail.

The first subrequest of the program—an *active:groovy*—generates a (pseudo)random UUID. Since we want to be able to get a new UUID at any time, we need to expire the response every time. The response of the subrequest is then assigned to the final response of our DPML program.

The second subrequest—an *active:modify-response*—modifies the headers of *this:response*, the final response of our DPML program. It does two things, it sets the mimetype of *this:response* to *text/plain* and the expiry time of *this:response* to 5 seconds (5000 milliseconds).

The net result is that, although we could potentially get a different UUID on any request, we will only get a different one every five seconds.

 The stumbling block for me was that I thought the *active:modify-response* subrequest would set the expiry of the *active:groovy* subrequest. It doesn't, but that only becomes clear if you think things through as I did here. In fact, the *active:modify-response* does for our DPML program what the *setExpiry* (and *setMimeType* and *setHeaders* and so on) does for the Groovy program.

DPML cannot *log*.

It can, however, handle a request that does the job, and an *active:log* tool is available.

```
<sequence>
  <literal assignment="afternoon" type="string">Good Afternoon</literal>
  <literal assignment="response" type="string">Good Evening</literal>
  <literal assignment="goodbye" type="string">Goodbye</literal>
  <request>
    <identifier>meta:dpml:log</identifier>
    <argument name="message">
      <literal type="string">%1, %2 and %3</literal>
    </argument>
    <argument name="param">this:afternoon</argument>
    <argument name="param">this:response</argument>
    <argument name="param">this:goodbye</argument>
  </request>
  <request assignment="response">
    <identifier>meta:dpml:modify-response</identifier>
    <argument name="operand">this:response</argument>
```

```
    <argument name="config">
      <literal type="xml">
        <config>
          <header name="mime">text/plain</header>
          <expiry method="CONSTANT">60000</expiry>
        </config>
      </literal>
    </argument>
  </request>
</sequence>
```

You can see the result in Figure 6-6.

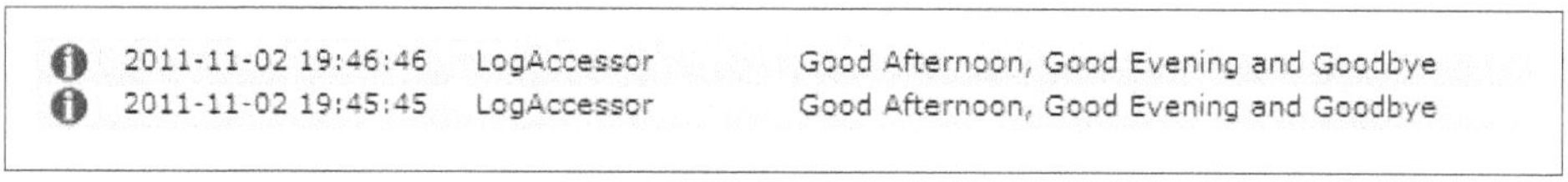

```
  ℹ   2011-11-02 19:46:46   LogAccessor        Good Afternoon, Good Evening and Goodbye
  ℹ   2011-11-02 19:45:45   LogAccessor        Good Afternoon, Good Evening and Goodbye
```

Figure 6-6. Loggings

The loggings can be found in the *NetKernel System Log* in Chapter 5, you can learn the why and how of logging in NetKernel. As you can see, the above program uses *active:modify-response* to avoid excessive logging.

By now, there are probably at least two things on your mind:

1. DPML is either argument heaven or argument hell.
2. There must be another way. In the *hello.dpml* program in Chapter 1, DPML logging is done differently!

```
<log>
  <message>
    <literal type="string">DPML example running with input %1</literal>
  </message>
  <param>arg:value</param>
<log>
```

It is the `<declare-tag>` tag that comes to the rescue.

```
<sequence>
  <declare-tag name="foreach">meta:ncode:builtin:foreach</declare-tag>
  <declare-tag name="tostring">meta:ncode:builtin:tostring</declare-tag>

  <foreach assignment="result">
    <collection>
      <request>
        <identifier>active:groovy</identifier>
        <argument name="operator">
          <literal type="string">
            context.createResponseFrom(0..4);
          </literal>
        </argument>
      </request>
    </collection>
    <do>
```

```
          <request>
            <identifier>active:groovy</identifier>
            <argument name="operator">
              <literal type="string">
                message=context.source("arg:item");
                context.createResponseFrom(message.toString());
              </literal>
            </argument>
            <argument name="item">foreach:item</argument>
          </request>
        </do>
      </foreach>

      <tostring assignment="response">
        <operand>this:result</operand>
      </tostring>
    </sequence>
```

Yes, that is the same example I used to explain the *active:ncodeForEach* tool, cleaned up, it seems. The request and identifier tags are replaced with the tag you declared; the attribute tags are replaced with their respective names.

Some of the more common tools have such an alias already defined for them in the DPML engine itself:

```
<if>
```
    meta:dpml:if

```
<throw>
```
    meta:dpml:throw

```
<exception>
```
    meta:dpml:exception

```
<modify-response>
```
    meta:dpml:modify-response

```
<log>
```
    meta:dpml:log

You can still have your own, though:

```
    <sequence>
      <declare-tag name="saycheese">meta:dpml:log</declare-tag>

      <literal assignment="afternoon" type="string">Good Afternoon</literal>
      <literal assignment="response" type="string">Good Evening</literal>
      <literal assignment="goodbye" type="string">Goodbye</literal>

      <saycheese>
        <message>
          <literal type="string">%1, %2 and %3</literal>
        </message>
        <param>this:afternoon</param>
        <param>this:response</param>
        <param>this:goodbye</param>
```

```
    </saycheese>

    <modify-response assignment="response">
      <operand>this:response</operand>
      <config>
        <literal type="xml">
          <config>
            <header name="mime">text/plain</header>
            <expiry method="CONSTANT">60000</expiry>
          </config>
        </literal>
      </config>
    </modify-response>
  </sequence>
```

Before you start shouting accusations, no, I am not a sadist, and I did not set things up to have a good laugh at your expense here!

What I did do was show you that DPML is indeed very lightweight and leverages all the available tools in exactly the same way. Only then did I add the syntax sugar that would have made you drown in tags earlier on.

Functional Programming

Functional Programming (*http://en.wikipedia.org/wiki/Functional_programming*) is going through quite a revival, making it from academia into commercial software development, which only proves that there are issues in software development that need solutions. The rest is economics. Whether functional programming will bring these solutions or not[2] remains to be seen.

Differences

DPML offers you the possibility to do functional programming. You could say (wrongly as you'll see in a minute) that to go from one to the other you replace *<sequence>* with *<closure>*.

```
<closure>
  <literal assignment="afternoon" type="string">Good Afternoon</literal>
  <literal assignment="response" type="string">Good Evening</literal>
  <literal assignment="goodbye" type="string">Goodbye</literal>
</closure>
```

My first reaction (as is probably yours) was, nice, but other than the fact that there is a second tag that can be used as the root element of a DPML program, this is the exact same program that explained *<sequence>*, and look, it does the same thing too.

---

2. I think NetKernel solves the issues, but you guessed that already, didn't you?

Wrong. It gives you the same response, but these two programs do completely different things. In order to prove that, here's two alternative programs. One with *<sequence>* and one with *<closure>*.

```
<sequence>
  <request assignment="afternoon">
    <identifier>active:groovy</identifier>
    <argument name="operator">
     <literal type="string">
       import org.netkernel.layer0.nkf.INKFResponse;
       println "Afternoon Groovy Program - Imperative";
       response = context.createResponseFrom("Good Afternoon");
       response.setExpiry(INKFResponse.EXPIRY_ALWAYS);
     </literal>
    </argument>
  </request>
  <request assignment="response">
    <identifier>active:groovy</identifier>
    <argument name="operator">
     <literal type="string">
       import org.netkernel.layer0.nkf.INKFResponse;
       println "Evening (response) Groovy Program - Imperative";
       response = context.createResponseFrom("Good Evening");
       response.setExpiry(INKFResponse.EXPIRY_ALWAYS);
     </literal>
    </argument>
  </request>
  <request assignment="goodbye">
    <identifier>active:groovy</identifier>
    <argument name="operator">
     <literal type="string">
       import org.netkernel.layer0.nkf.INKFResponse;
       println "Goodbye Groovy Program - Imperative";
       response = context.createResponseFrom("Goodbye");
       response.setExpiry(INKFResponse.EXPIRY_ALWAYS);
     </literal>
    </argument>
  </request>
</sequence>

<closure>
  <request assignment="afternoon">
    <identifier>active:groovy</identifier>
    <argument name="operator">
     <literal type="string">
       import org.netkernel.layer0.nkf.INKFResponse;
       println "Afternoon Groovy Program - Functional";
       response = context.createResponseFrom("Good Afternoon");
       response.setExpiry(INKFResponse.EXPIRY_ALWAYS);
     </literal>
    </argument>
  </request>
  <request assignment="response">
    <identifier>active:groovy</identifier>
    <argument name="operator">
```

```
        <literal type="string">
          import org.netkernel.layer0.nkf.INKFResponse;
          println "Evening (response) Groovy Program - Functional";
          response = context.createResponseFrom("Good Evening");
          response.setExpiry(INKFResponse.EXPIRY_ALWAYS);
        </literal>
      </argument>
    </request>
    <request assignment="goodbye">
      <identifier>active:groovy</identifier>
      <argument name="operator">
        <literal type="string">
          import org.netkernel.layer0.nkf.INKFResponse;
          println "Goodbye Groovy Program - Functional";
          response = context.createResponseFrom("Goodbye");
          response.setExpiry(INKFResponse.EXPIRY_ALWAYS);
        </literal>
      </argument>
    </request>
  </closure>
```

It makes no difference, you say? Did you look at the console log, by any chance
(Figure 6-7)?

```
Afternoon Groovy Program - Imperative
Evening (response) Groovy Program - Imperative
Goodbye Groovy Program - Imperative
Evening (response) Groovy Program - Functional
```

Figure 6-7. Console log

A sequence will execute in order. In this case, that means three requests. A closure will
execute whatever satisfies its needs. A root element closure needs a final response, so
it fires the request that delivers that, and only that request.

Now, that requires a whole other approach to coding. To make things more complex,
you can have sequences inside closures and closures inside sequences. You can have
referenced closures (executed because they deliver a value that is consumed) and *requested closures* (executed when called; the equivalent of what an imperative developer
thinks a function is).

 To speak up for imperative programming, in most (if not all) *compiled*
languages, the compilation will optimize dead (and other useless) code
out of the end result. And some of the more fancy editors will indicate
and do away with dead and other useless code. Still, with scripting (in-
terpreted) languages moving to the front lines, there is definitely something to say for the functional approach.

More Information

I am not a functional programmer. Learning the functional approach is on my to-do list since I noticed Clojure is available in NetKernel, but I didn't get there yet (I had to write a book and stuff; you know how it is).

Now, while I could cook up some examples (or steal the ones from the NetKernel documentation), there would not be any added value to them, nothing for you to learn from my experience. So, what I'm going to do is point you to the relevant documentation in NetKernel and keep quiet myself.

In the NetKernel documentation, there is a DPML guide (which you can find for yourself). The relevant points you want to take a look at are *Closure*, *Import*, and the *Sequential versus Functional* example.

 In that (otherwise excellent) example, I do not agree with the algorithm that follows the *"To convert sequential to functional, simply apply the following algorithm"* line. While the algorithm will no doubt give you the correct result (and is much better than my own *"replace sequence with closure"*), I'm quite certain functional programming in NetKernel cannot and should not be reduced to that.

Conclusion

I hope that I've shown you that while you cannot do anything with DPML, it is a versatile and useful language.[3]It was the composition language of choice of many NetKernel 3 users (regardless of their own programming backgrounds), and while the new DPML 2.0 release has yet to gain the same popularity, everything you need is there and ready to roll.

I did go through most of the language, but I didn't go into every little detail. By all means, go through the guide in the NetKernel documentation. At least it should make a whole lot more sense now.

If I haven't convinced you of the true power yet, check out Chapter 8, where you can see DPML in a completely different light.[4]

---

3. And if you agree with me that this is not a contradiction, I have succeeded.

4. If I have convinced you, join us, for nCoDE is an amazing tool.

XRL

The *XML Recursion Language*, or XRL, is a declarative language that supports the modular composition of structured XML documents.

How wonderful, isn't it? If you understood that snippet from the NetKernel documentation, move on to the stuff below. If you didn't, let me tell you that XRL (and its young sister TRL, Text Recursion Language) is the tool you want to have mastered when somebody asks you, "So what can you actually do with this NetKernel thingie, and why is it different from everything else?"

Prerequisites

You should have completed Part I. Chapters in this part do not follow a specific order and do not build upon each other, but the basics should be known by now.

Setup

The *Scripting Playpen* is going to be the theatre of operations, and DPML is the language of choice for the examples, but we need to be able to pull in extra resources (which is in fact the whole point of XRL). A small file serving module will do the trick.

The Design

We've seen the required pattern earlier on in this book, in Chapter 3 in fact, where we map the ExtJS libraries. These are the elements:

1. Requests will be of the form *res:/chapter7/*.
2. Requests get mapped to the data directory of the module.
3. The module is provided with documentation and unittest.

The Code

Example 7-1. module.xml

```xml
<?xml version="1.0" encoding="UTF-8"?>
<module version="2.0">
  <meta>
    <identity>
      <uri>urn:org:netkernelbook:chapter7:fileserver</uri>
      <version>1.0.0</version>
    </identity>
    <info>
      <name>Chapter 7 File Server</name>
      <description>NetKernelbook Chapter 7 File Server</description>
    </info>
  </meta>

  <system>
    <dynamic/>
  </system>

  <rootspace
    name="Chapter 7 File Server"
    public="true"
    uri="urn:org:netkernelbook:chapter7:fileserver">
    <fileset>
      <regex>res:/chapter7/(.*)</regex>
      <rewrite>res:/data/$1</rewrite>
    </fileset>
  </rootspace>

  <rootspace
    name="Chapter 7 File Server - Documentation"
    public="true"
    uri="urn:org:netkernelbook:chapter7:fileserver:documentation">
    <fileset>
      <regex>res:/etc/system/(Books|Docs).xml</regex>
    </fileset>

    <fileset>
      <regex>res:/resources/documentation/.*</regex>
    </fileset>
  </rootspace>

  <rootspace
    name="Chapter 7 File Server - Unit Test"
    public="true"
    uri="urn:org:netkernelbook:chapter7:fileserver:unittest">
    <fileset>
      <regex>res:/etc/system/Tests.xml</regex>
    </fileset>

    <fileset>
      <regex>res:/resources/unittest/.*</regex>
    </fileset>
```

```
    <endpoint>
      <prototype>Limiter</prototype>
      <grammar>res:/etc/
        <regex type="anything"/>
      </grammar>
    </endpoint>

    <import>
      <uri>urn:org:netkernelbook:chapter7:fileserver</uri>
    </import>

    <import>
      <uri>urn:org:netkernel:ext:layer1</uri>
    </import>
  </rootspace>
</module>
```

With *module.xml* in place, we can implement the basics for the module.

Example 7-2. Directory layout

```
data
  testfile.txt
etc
  system
    Books.xml
    Docs.xml
    Tests.xml
resources
  documentation
    doc_guide.txt
  unittest
    testlist.xml
module.xml
```

Let us take that from the top down.

Example 7-3. testfile.txt

```
this is a testfile containing text
```

As you can deduce from *module.xml*, the data directory is where you will put the files/ directories that you want served. To start with only *testfile.txt* is in that location. We'll use it for the unittest.

Example 7-4. Books.xml

```
<?xml version="1.0" encoding="UTF-8"?>
<books>
  <book>
    <id>book:urn:org:netkernelbook:chapter7:fileserver</id>
    <title>Chapter 7 File Server</title>
    <desc>netkernelbook chapter7 file server documentation</desc>
    <toc>
```

```
      <item id="urn:org:netkernelbook:chapter7:fileserver:guide"/>
    </toc>
  </book>
</books>
```

Example 7-5. Docs.xml

```
<?xml version="1.0" encoding="UTF-8"?>
<docs>
  <doc>
    <id>urn:org:netkernelbook:chapter7:fileserver:guide</id>
    <title>Guide to Chapter 7 File Server</title>
    <desc>chapter 7 file server explained</desc>
    <uri>res:/resources/documentation/doc_guide.txt</uri>
  </doc>
</docs>
```

Even a module that doesn't contain a lot in the way of coding needs documentation.
Books.xml and *Docs.xml* set that up.

Example 7-6. Tests.xml

```
<?xml version="1.0" encoding="UTF-8"?>
<tests>
  <test>
    <id>test:urn:org:netkernelbook:chapter7:fileserver</id>
    <name>Chapter 7 File Server</name>
    <desc>netkernelbook chapter7 file server unittest</desc>
    <uri>res:/resources/unittest/testlist.xml</uri>
  </test>
</tests>
```

The same goes for testing. With *Tests.xml*, we plug into NetKernel's test framework.

Example 7-7. doc_guide.txt

```
= Chapter 7 File Server =

== Details ==
Request gets the equivalent file in the '''data''' subdirectory. This module is for
internal use only and thus not exposed on the Frontend HTTPFulcrum.

== General Request ==
res:/chapter7/.*

For more information on editing documentation
see the [doc:sysadmin:guide:doc:editing|Editing Guide].
```

The actual documentation is short and to the point.

Example 7-8. testlist.xml

```
<?xml version="1.0" encoding="UTF-8"?>
<testlist>
  <test name="simple text file request">
    <request>
```

```
      <identifier>res:/chapter7/testfile.txt</identifier>
      <representation>java.lang.String</representation>
      <verb>SOURCE</verb>
    </request>
    <assert>
      <stringEquals>this is a testfile containing text</stringEquals>
    </assert>
  </test>
</testlist>
```

Does *testfile.txt* contain the string mentioned? We need no more to test the functionality of our module.

Verify and Troubleshoot

To check if the module works is easy, just run the unittest (Figure 7-1).

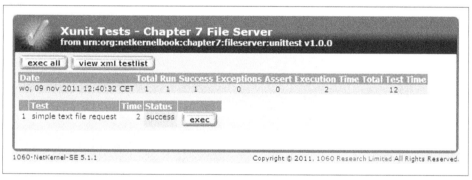

Figure 7-1. Unittest

In case things are not working for you, here are the most common reasons:

- Did you add the new module to *[installroot]/etc/modules.xml*? I didn't tell you to, as I assume you know by now.
- Does the *testfile.txt* file contain just the single line (without newline at the end)? It has to match exactly, or the test will fail.

Integrate in Scripting Playpen

With a place for the extra resources in place, we need to make them available in the *Scripting Playpen*.

Yes, that means we are going to change one of the base NetKernel modules. Why not? Once you become a bit proficient, it pays to study those modules, and what good is studying if you can't or don't change anything?

Copy and Rename

Copy the complete *[installroot]/modules/urn.org.netkernel.ext.introspect-xx.yy.zz* directory to a new *[installroot]/modules/urn.org.netkernel.ext.introspect-xx.yy.(zz+1)* directory.

 If the original is not a directory but a jar (it is not at this moment in time, but it can be in the future), unpack the jar to a directory, and rename that.

Changes

Make the *following changes* in the *module.xml* of the new introspect directory. By the way—in case it is not obvious—you need to replace xx.yy.(zz+1) with the current (+1) version number of the introspect module. I have no way of knowing what that number will be at the time you read this (it is 1.38.29 at this time).

```
<module version="2.0">
  <meta>
    <identity>
      ...
      <version>xx.yy.(zz+1)</version>
    </identity>
    ...
  </meta>
  ...
  <system>
    <dynamic/>
  </system>
  ...
  <rootspace uri="spp:inner" private-filter="false" public="true" name="Scripting
Playpen Inner">
    ...
    <import>
      <uri>urn:org:netkernelbook:chapter7:fileserver</uri>
      <private/>
    </import>

    <endpoint>
      <prototype>DynamicImport</prototype>
      <config>active:FindLanguageRuntimes</config>
      <private/>
    </endpoint>
  </rootspace>
</module>
```

Activation

As you know, multiple versions of a module can coexist. However, that is not a good idea for a module exposed to a fulcrum. You'll find out what it means to *see everything twice*[1] if both introspect modules are active (by all means, try it though; if you got this

---

far, you shouldn't be scared of messing things up anymore). Change the *following* in *[installroot]/etc/modules.xml* to disable the old module and activate the changed one:

```
<modules>
  ...
  <disabled runlevel="2">modules/urn.org.netkernel.ext.introspect-xx.yy.zz/</disabled
>
  <module runlevel="2">modules/urn.org.netkernel.ext.introspect-xx.yy.(zz+1)/</
module>
  ...
</modules>
```

Basics

XRL recursively replaces resource identifiers with their resource representations in a valid XML document. The end result and all intermediate results have to be valid XML as well.

There's definitely more to it than that, but that definition will serve for a start. If you are familiar with the W3C XML technologies, then an advanced *XML Inclusions* is a good way to start thinking about XRL.

Humble Beginnings

We are going to execute DPML (= valid XML) code but with part of the code pulled in from elsewhere. That elsewhere is, of course, the module we created earlier on in this chapter. Create the *following file* in the *[moduleroot]/data* directory.

Example 7-9. template01.xml

```
<?xml version="1.0" encoding="UTF-8"?>
<config xmlns:xrl="http://netkernel.org/xrl">
  <header name="mime">text/plain</header>
  <expiry method="CONSTANT">60000</expiry>
</config>
```

We don't even need XRL to pull in the template. Try the following DPML in the *Scripting Playpen.*

```
<sequence>
  <request assignment="response">
    <identifier>active:groovy</identifier>
    <argument name="operator">
      <literal type="string">
        import org.netkernel.layer0.nkf.INKFResponse;

        myUUID   = UUID.randomUUID().toString();
        response = context.createResponseFrom(myUUID);
```

---

1. *Catch-22*, Joseph Heller, 1961, ISBN 978-1-45162-665-0.

```
        response.setExpiry(INKFResponse.EXPIRY_ALWAYS);
      </literal>
    </argument>
  </request>
  <request assignment="response">
    <identifier>meta:dpml:modify-response</identifier>
    <argument name="operand">this:response</argument>
    <argument name="config">res:/chapter7/template01.xml</argument>
  </request>
</sequence>
```

Do note the following attribute in the root tag of our template though:

```
xmlns:xrl="http://netkernel.org/xrl"
```

The template has to be *valid XML*, and the XRL tags inside the template (which we'll have in the next example) require the *XRL namespace*.

Recursive Replacement

We are going to execute DPML (= valid XML) code but with part of the code pulled in from elsewhere. And the code that we pull in does itself pull a code from elsewhere. Potentially this can go on as deep as you wish. <u>Create</u> the *following file* in the *[moduleroot]/data* directory.

Example 7-10. template02.xml

```
<?xml version="1.0" encoding="UTF-8"?>
<config xmlns:xrl="http://netkernel.org/xrl">
  <header name="mime">text/plain</header>
  <xrl:include>
    <xrl:identifier>res:/chapter7/expiry02.xml</xrl:identifier>
  </xrl:include>
</config>
```

As you can see, just specifying the resource in DPML will not be sufficient in this case, for our template includes another resource. <u>Create</u> the *following file* in the *[moduleroot]/data* directory.

 And that is enough repetition. For the rest of this chapter, I'll assume you know where to create the mentioned files: that's right, in the chapter 7 *[moduleroot]/data* directory.

Example 7-11. expiry02.xml

```
<expiry method="CONSTANT">60000</expiry>
```

<u>Try</u> the following DPML in the *Scripting Playpen* to see how it works.

```
<sequence>
  <request assignment="response">
```

```
    <identifier>active:groovy</identifier>
    <argument name="operator">
      <literal type="string">
        import org.netkernel.layer0.nkf.INKFResponse;

        myUUID   = UUID.randomUUID().toString();
        response = context.createResponseFrom(myUUID);

        response.setExpiry(INKFResponse.EXPIRY_ALWAYS);
      </literal>
    </argument>
  </request>
  <request assignment="response">
    <identifier>meta:dpml:modify-response</identifier>
    <argument name="operand">this:response</argument>
    <argument name="config">
      <request>
        <identifier>meta:XRL2Runtime</identifier>
        <argument name="template">res:/chapter7/template02.xml</argument>
      </request>
    </argument>
  </request>
</sequence>
```

Dynamic Recursive Replacement

The above is all there is to XRL, no more. True, there is some syntax to be mastered, but this is the basic functionality. Not impressive, you say? Well, to finish off the basics, let me show you how to make things more dynamic. Here's the template:

Example 7-12. template03.xml

```
<?xml version="1.0" encoding="UTF-8"?>
<config xmlns:xrl="http://netkernel.org/xrl">
  <header name="mime">text/plain</header>
  <xrl:include>
    <xrl:identifier>arg:expiry</xrl:identifier>
  </xrl:include>
</config>
```

Try the following DPML in the *Scripting Playpen*.

```
<sequence>
  <request assignment="response">
    <identifier>active:groovy</identifier>
    <argument name="operator">
      <literal type="string">
        import org.netkernel.layer0.nkf.INKFResponse;

        myUUID   = UUID.randomUUID().toString();
        response = context.createResponseFrom(myUUID);

        response.setExpiry(INKFResponse.EXPIRY_ALWAYS);
      </literal>
```

```
        </argument>
      </request>
      <request assignment="response">
        <identifier>meta:dpml:modify-response</identifier>
        <argument name="operand">this:response</argument>
        <argument name="config">
          <request>
            <identifier>meta:XRL2Runtime</identifier>
            <argument name="template">res:/chapter7/template03.xml</argument>
            <argument name="expiry">res:/chapter7/expiry02.xml</argument>
          </request>
        </argument>
      </request>
    </sequence>
```

Suddenly, a fixed resource request has become an argument. You do not understand? Add the *following file*, and I'll explain:

Example 7-13. expiry03.xml

```
<expiry method="CONSTANT">10000</expiry>
```

Now, change back and forth between these two definitions for the expiry argument:

```
        <argument name="expiry">res:/chapter7/expiry02.xml</argument>
```

```
        <argument name="expiry">res:/chapter7/expiry03.xml</argument>
```

If the *expiry02.xml* file is used, timeout of the UUID is 60 seconds. If the *expiry03.xml* file is used, timeout of the UUID is 10 seconds.

That is not dynamic, you say, because I explicitly state the file in the DPML program? Well, it's an example (a contrived one at that), and . . . OK, OK, let me revise the template and the program a bit.

Example 7-14. template04.xml

```
<?xml version="1.0" encoding="UTF-8"?>
<config xmlns:xrl="http://netkernel.org/xrl">
  <header name="mime">text/plain</header>
  <xrl:include>
    <xrl:identifier>res:/chapter7/expiry0[[arg:expiry]].xml</xrl:identifier>
  </xrl:include>
</config>
```

Try the following DPML in the *Scripting Playpen*.

```
    <sequence>
      <request assignment="response">
        <identifier>active:groovy</identifier>
        <argument name="operator">
          <literal type="string">
            import org.netkernel.layer0.nkf.INKFResponse;

            myUUID   = UUID.randomUUID().toString();
            response = context.createResponseFrom(myUUID);
```

```
        response.setExpiry(INKFResponse.EXPIRY_ALWAYS);
      </literal>
    </argument>
  </request>
  <request assignment="response">
    <identifier>meta:dpml:modify-response</identifier>
    <argument name="operand">this:response</argument>
    <argument name="config">
      <request>
        <identifier>meta:XRL2Runtime</identifier>
        <argument name="template">res:/chapter7/template04.xml</argument>
        <argument name="expiry">3</argument>
      </request>
    </argument>
  </request>
</sequence>
```

There you have it. Pass 2 and you'll get a 60-second expiry, pass 3 and you'll get a 10-second expiry. Having covered arguments to the XRL runtime as well, we can now safely move on to somewhat more complex things.

Three Ways to Use XRL

There are three XRL processing tags, each covering another type of replacement.

xrl:include

This is the recursive *XML Inclusions* tag. You include valid xml at either the exact location of the *xrl:include* or at a specified (xpath) location.

The example that follows serves for all three tags, so don't worry if it all doesn't make sense right away. Here are the files:

Example 7-15. template05.xml

```
<?xml version="1.0" encoding="UTF-8"?>
<sequence xmlns:xrl="http://netkernel.org/xrl">
  <xrl:include>
    <xrl:xpath>../../sequence</xrl:xpath>
    <xrl:identifier>[[arg:program]]</xrl:identifier>
  </xrl:include>
</sequence>
```

Example 7-16. program.dpml

```
<sequence xmlns:xrl="http://netkernel.org/xrl">
  <literal assignment="afternoon" type="string">Good Afternoon</literal>
  <literal assignment="response" type="xml">
    <xrl:include>
      <xrl:identifier>res:/chapter7/goodevening.html</xrl:identifier>
    </xrl:include>
  </literal>
```

```
    <literal assignment="goodbye" type="string">Goodbye</literal>
</sequence>
```

Example 7-17. goodevening.html

```
<html xmlns:xrl="http://netkernel.org/xrl">
  <body>
    <h1/>
    <xrl:eval>
      <xrl:xpath>../h1</xrl:xpath>
      <xrl:identifier>res:/chapter7/goodevening.txt</xrl:identifier>
    </xrl:eval>
    <div>
      <a href="">Chapter 7 Testfile</a>
      <xrl:resolve>
        <xrl:xpath>../a/@href</xrl:xpath>
        <xrl:identifier>res:/chapter7/testfile.txt</xrl:identifier>
      </xrl:resolve>
    </div>
  </body>
</html>
```

Example 7-18. goodevening.txt

```
Good Evening!
```

<u>Try</u> the following DPML in the *Scripting Playpen*.

```
    <sequence>
      <request assignment="response">
        <identifier>meta:DPMLRuntime</identifier>
        <argument name="operator">
          <request>
            <identifier>meta:XRL2Runtime</identifier>
            <argument name="template">res:/chapter7/template05.xml</argument>
            <argument name="program">res:/chapter7/program.dpml</argument>
          </request>
        </argument>
      </request>
      <request assignment="response">
        <identifier>meta:dpml:modify-response</identifier>
        <argument name="operand">this:response</argument>
        <argument name="config">
          <literal type="xml">
            <config>
              <header name="mime">text/html</header>
              <expiry method="CONSTANT">5000</expiry>
            </config>
          </literal>
        </argument>
      </request>
    </sequence>
```

I now want to prime your mind with the words *code generator*. There, done.

This is *what happens* when you <u>select</u> *execute* in the *Scripting Playpen*:

1. The DPML is executed.
2. The first step of the DPML program is the execution of another DPML program (meta:DPMLRuntime). The second step modifies the response so we can see the output correctly (as HTML), but it plays no further part in the XRL story.
3. The operator (DPML code to be executed) of the first step is determined through an XRL request.
4. The XRL uses a template (*template05.xml*) and gets passed a program-argument.
5. Inside the template *xrl:include* triggers a replace of the sequence with what it pulls from the identifier formed by the program argument (*program.dpml*).
6. In turn the program has an *xrl:include* to pull in another resource (*goodevening.html*).

xrl:resolve

Have you ever wondered how to provide a clickable link to a ROC resource in an HTML page? This tag does the resolving and provides the URI. And so, we can continue the *what happens* list.

7. The HTML resource has a link to the testfile resource. The *xrl:include* does that for us.

Question: so, these links will change if the implementation of the endpoint changes? Answer: absolutely!

xrl:eval

Next to tags covered by *xrl:include*, an XML document is mainly made up of text. This tag allows for manipulation of text, and allows us to finish the *what happens* list.

8. The *xrl:eval* sets the *text* of the h1 tag to what it finds in a given resource.

Question: instead of a file resource, could I have a *freemarker* (call) resource here with a dynamic text template? Answer: absolutely.

Figure 7-2. XRL tags

All Three Together

The most common pitfall for XRL is that you overcomplicate matters, as did I for the above example. But otherwise, knock yourself (and the people you are trying to impress) out with all this dynamic stuff.

In Figure 7-2, you can see what the result of the execution will look like, more or less, depending on the browser you use.

Actually, more interesting is the source code of the web page in your browser. That should look like this:

```
<html>
  <body>
    <h1>Good Evening!</h1>
    <div>
      <a href="/chapter7/testfile.txt">Chapter 7 Testfile</a>
    </div>
  </body>
</html>
```

It looks nice, doesn't it? Figure 7-3 shows what you get when you <u>select</u> the *link*.

It looks like *xrl:resolve* did not do its job. Or did it? Well, since this is an advanced chapter, all I'm going to tell you is that *xrl:resolve* did do its job and that it is trivial to get the link to work. The how and why you should be able to find yourself, and only after you found it yourself can you verify the answer in Appendix F.

Did You/I Notice?

You are no doubt burning with desire to try some XRL stuff yourself now. Before you do, there are some things I want to bring to your attention.

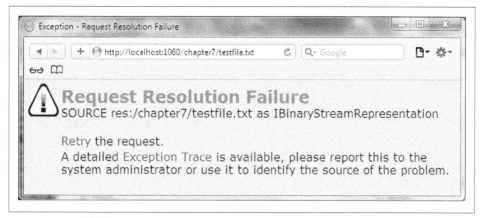

Figure 7-3. Link fail

Did you notice that the *xrl:identifier* tag (inside *xrl:include*, *xrl:resolve*, *xrl:eval*) looks remarkably like an identifier tag (inside a request)? The reason is, of course, that you are doing a request, and you can pass arguments to that request as well with *xrl:argument* tags.

Yes, I did notice that more compact forms of the three XRL processing tags exist. By all means, check the documentation for their use. Like in the DPML chapter, I'd rather have you walk steadily first before going into typing optimizations.

Quite recently, XRL got a little sister, the *Text Recursion Language* or TRL. TRL compares to Freemarker as XRL compares to XSLT. Freemarker and XSLT are template engines; TRL and XRL add the ROC layer to those engines. Yes, they can, (and I did so in this chapter), but more often than not, you'll find them paired.

Conclusion

Next to the *module.xml* files, there is no place where the true spirit of ROC shines through so much as when using XRL.

The download for this chapter can be found here (*http://dl.dropbox.com/u/65770556/urn.org.netkernelbook.chapter7.fileserver-1.0.0.zip*).

nCoDE

If you compare the number of code listings with the number of screenshots in this book, you might conclude that NetKernel is not a GUI-based development tool. I agree.

The *NetKernel Compositional Development Environment* is the exception to the rule. It provides you with a visual editor to compose endpoints. In that it has the same function as DPML and indeed, behind the gui layer nCoDE translates to DPML. So, you could call it a *visual DPML*.

I was very skeptical about it. I've seen my share of GUI tools that are supposed to aid and mostly only succeed in getting in the way. I have another opinion about nCoDE, but I'm not going to force that on you. I'll let you form your own opinion.

Prerequisites

You should have completed Part I. Chapters in this part do not follow a specific order and do not build upon each other, but the basics should be known by now.

Beginnings

nCoDE endpoints can be added into any module, but in order to have a clean slate, we'll make a new one.

Example 8-1. module.xml

```
<?xml version="1.0" encoding="UTF-8"?>
<module version="2.0">
  <meta>
    <identity>
      <uri>urn:org:netkernelbook:chapter8:ncode</uri>
      <version>1.0.0</version>
    </identity>
    <info>
      <name>Chapter 8 nCoDE</name>
      <description>NetKernelbook Chapter 8 nCoDE</description>
```

```
      </info>
  </meta>

  <system>
    <dynamic/>
  </system>

  <rootspace
    name="Chapter 8 nCoDE"
    public="true"
    uri="urn:org:netkernelbook:chapter8:ncode">
    <fileset>
      <regex>res:/etc/system/SimpleDynamicImportHook.xml</regex>
    </fileset>

    <endpoint>
      <name>Chapter 8 nCoDE Endpoints</name>
      <prototype>nCoDERuntime</prototype>
      <operator>res:/resources/endpoints/ncode-state.xml</operator>
    </endpoint>

    <!-- Mutable fileset to save the nCoDE programs         -->
    <fileset>
      <regex>res:/resources/endpoints/.*</regex>
      <mutable>true</mutable>
      <poll>100</poll>
      <private/>
    </fileset>

    <!-- Needed for the nCoDERuntime prototype              -->
    <import>
      <uri>urn:org:netkernel:lang:ncode</uri>
      <private/>
    </import>

    <!-- Underneath here come the imports of the tools you   -->
    <!-- want to use.                                        -->
  </rootspace>
</module>
```

So, what is needed is an instance of the nCoDERuntime prototype with a resource in a mutable fileset.

I added the main rootspace to the Frontend HTTPFulcrum. Strictly speaking, this is not necessary; you could develop nCoDE endpoints that are imported elsewhere. It makes things easier to test for this chapter, though.

With the above information, you should be able to create and activate the module. Do so.

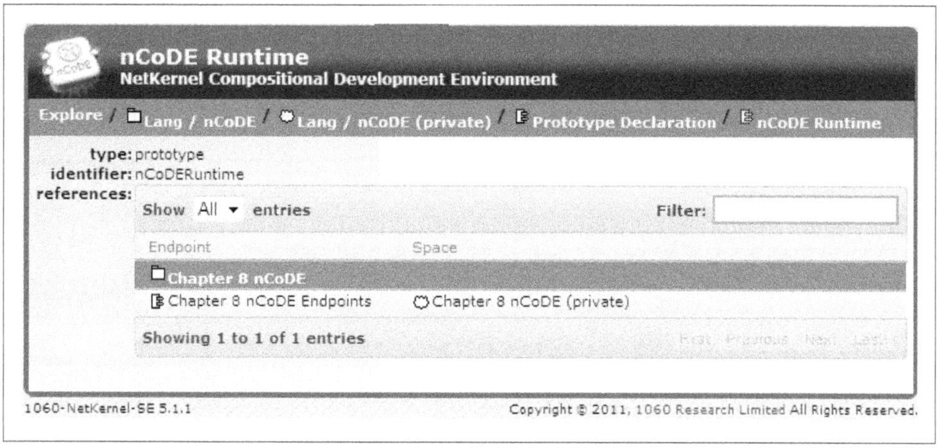

Figure 8-1. nCoDE Instances

 You don't have to create the *ncode-state.xml* file. Just the directory structure will do. Thanks to the mutable fileset, nCoDE will take care of the file itself.

When your module is up and running, point *your browser* at *http://localhost:1060/ panel/urn:org:netkernel:nkse:control:panel:explorer*, and select *nCoDE Instances*. Unless you already had other nCoDE modules, the result should look like Figure 8-1.

Select the *Chapter 8 nCoDE Endpoints* physical endpoint and you'll find yourself in the nCoDE editor (Figure 8-2).

We'll quickly develop a *hello world* example to show the warp and woof of the editor. Select the *plus sign (+)* at the bottom of the editor view.

You should have gotten a canvas with a response labeled *endpoint1*. Before we start filling the canvas, we should change the properties of the endpoint. Select the *endpoint1 label*.

Change the following *properties* (see Figure 8-3):

1. The name from *endpoint1* to *helloWorld*.
2. The id from *chapter8:ncode:endpoint1* to *chapter8:ncode:helloWorld*.
3. The grammar can be a full-blown grammar. The named groups can be used as arguments further on. As you can see, we get a message argument from the grammar.

```
<group>res:/chapter8/ncode/helloWorld/
  <group name="message">
    <regex type="anything"/>
  </group>
</group>
```

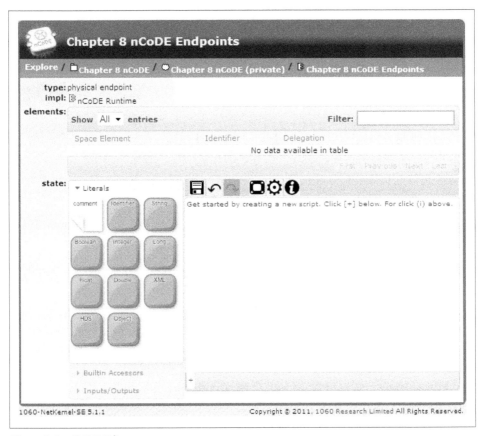

Figure 8-2. nCoDE Editor

<u>Select</u> *OK* to keep the settings and close the properties window.

<u>Select</u> the *Inputs/Outputs palette* (see Figure 8-4).

If you entered the grammar correctly, you should see an *arg:message* element. Drag a copy onto the canvas and resize (bottom right of the element) it a bit so the name fits (Figure 8-5).

What remains to be done is pretty obvious: <u>connect</u> the *dots* and <u>select</u> the *disk icon* to save (the changes to) the endpoint (Figure 8-6)!

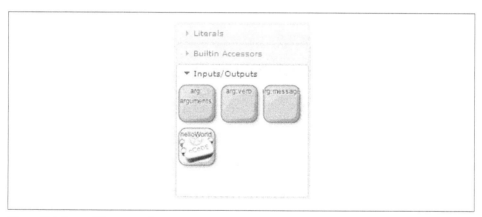

Figure 8-3. Endpoint properties

Figure 8-4. Inputs/Outputs palette

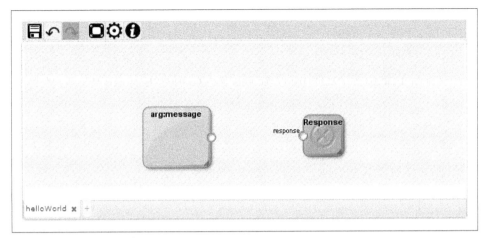

Figure 8-5. arg:message element

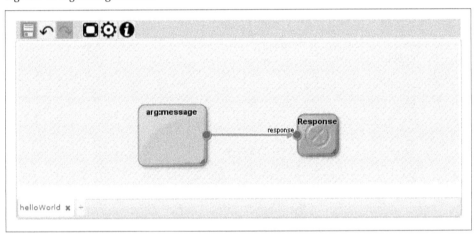

Figure 8-6. Connect the dots

Notice that once the connection is made, the response element changes color (from red to grey) since its requirements are fulfilled.

<u>Point</u> *another browser window* at *http://localhost:8080/chapter8/ncode/helloWorld/My %20Message.*

Nice, is it not? We defined the *helloWorld* endpoint (and can define as many others as we like) inside the chapter 8 nCoDE runtime, and it works as if we had specified it in the *module.xml.*

As an exercise, remove the *arg:message* element (select an element or connection, and a remove button will appear), and replace it with a *string* element from the Literals palette.

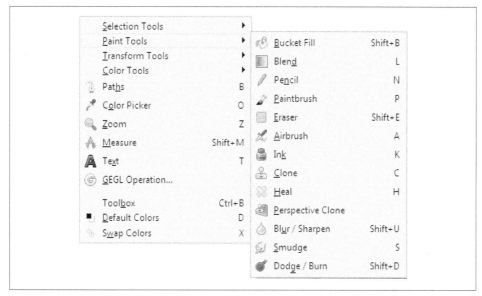

Figure 8-7. Gimp palette

Elements from the Literals palette have an editable value. Select them to enter it.

Give Me More

The tools menu from Gimp (Figure 8-7) has a lot more options than our—I admit it—somewhat meager palette in nCoDE.

Think: how would we normally inform a module that we want to use, for example, Freemarker? We would do it by importing the Freemarker module in the relevant root-space in *module.xml*.

Add the *following imports* in the chapter 8 nCoDE rootspace.

```
<!-- Underneath here come the tools you want to use    -->
<import>
  <uri>urn:org:netkernel:lang:ncode:builtins</uri>
  <private/>
</import>
<import>
  <uri>urn:org:netkernel:lang:freemarker</uri>
  <private/>
</import>
```

After the chapter 8 nCoDE module reloads, you should see a couple of changes in the nCoDE editor.

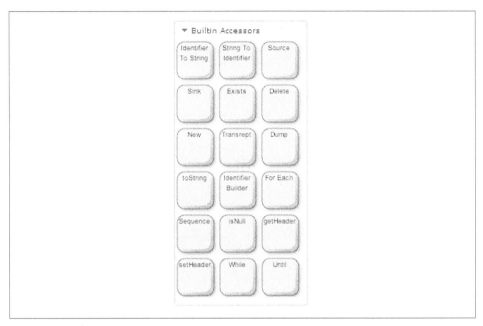

Figure 8-8. Built-in Accessors

Figure 8-9. Accessors

The palette of *Built-in Accessors* (see Figure 8-8) has grown substantially—guess from which of the imports the new elements come—and a new palette has appeared, *Accessors*.

Do you see (Figure 8-9)? By importing the Freemarker module, we now get access to it in nCoDE.

Actually, it is not only the import. The module we import has to export the endpoints it wants to make available for nCoDE import. How? By exposing */etc/system/CDEPalette.xml*. For Freemarker, that file looks like:

```
<palette>
  <endpoint id="freemarker:runtime" group="other" />
</palette>
```

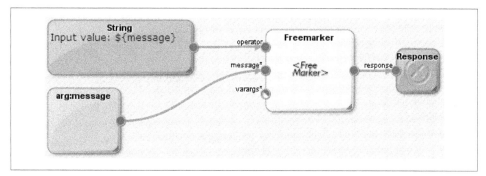

Figure 8-10. First Module

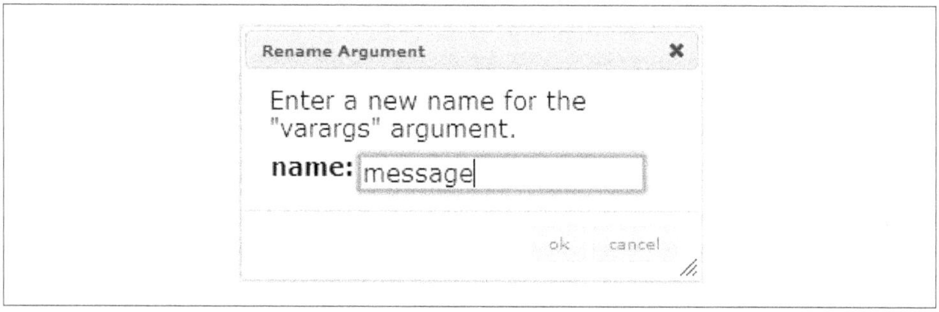

Rename Argument   ✕

Enter a new name for the
"varargs" argument.

name: message

ok   cancel

Figure 8-11. Varargs

Now, let us make the nCoDE *helloWorld* look a bit more like the original *firstmodule* one. Figure 8-10 shows how.

You should be able to manage that on your own, except maybe the message argument on the Freemarker element side. Doesn't your Freemarker element have a message argument? Well, neither does mine. But it does have a varargs argument that allows for multiple connections. Connect the *arg:message* element output (in ROC terms, *the representation of the resource*) to the varargs argument of the Freemarker element, and another varargs connection point will show up. And on top of that, you can change the name of connection points indicated with * (an asterisk). See Figure 8-11.

It Is Not a Toy

While I advocate testing throughout this book, it is not something I enjoy a lot. And things I do not enjoy, I tend to *forget*. Recently I was working on a LZMA accessor. Now, compression algorithms have to be tested thoroughly. And then a use for nCoDE (which I had not looked at properly until then) came to mind (see Figure 8-12).

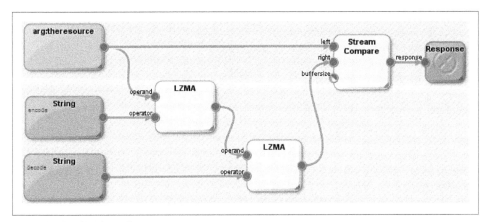

Figure 8-12. LZMA verify

I whipped that up in seconds, in true ROC everything-is-a-resource fashion. A second thought swiftly followed the first one: I didn't have to do this myself. I could give it to a team specialized in testing, and they wouldn't have to know about programming.

The third thought bubble must surely sound obvious to you, but until that moment I approached nCoDE with a typical sysadmin attitude.[1] Then all of a sudden, I was no longer looking at a mere toy but at the first graphical development/composition tool worth its salt (for me), one that could be seeded with tools and then given to somebody knowing the business: an end user. OK, still a technically savvy one, and maybe I'd have to sit next to him and communicate with him, but wouldn't that do both our souls a bit of good?

If you are not impressed by now, Figure 8-13 is what I made a couple of minutes after the above *lzma verify* endpoint. To understand it, you have to know that nCoDE endpoints can be made available to other nCoDE prototype-containing modules (through export in */etc/system/CDEPalette.xml*) and that within the same nCoDE prototype endpoint, all endpoints are visible and usable in the Inputs/Outputs palette.

So, I started a new endpoint, pulled *lzma verify* from the Inputs/Outputs palette, wrapped it in a *For Each* loop, and gave it a collection of identifiers as input. The output will be a collection of values from the *Stream Compare* inside *lzma verify*. In other words, the response of this tool will be a test report of the *lzma* utility with different inputs. Again, in other words, all I've got left to do is prepare the different inputs that will guarantee me *lzma* works correctly, and I've got a complete test battery in no time.

---

1. Give me root and vi, and I'll finish the job.

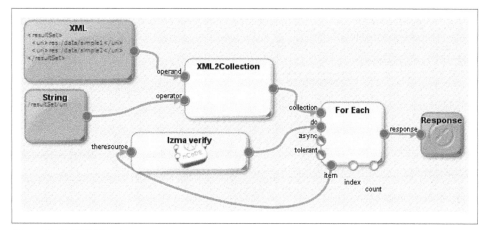

Figure 8-13. *LZMA unittest*

Figure 8-14. *helloWorldActive*

Ahead of Myself

The examples in the previous section are somewhat ahead of what we did ourselves so far. I'll rectify that in this section where we'll develop our very own *helloWorld* test battery.

helloWorldActive

In a first step, we are going to provide an active grammar for our *helloWorld* endpoint. This makes it easier to put it inside a test battery.

 I'm just voicing a personal opinion when I say that *REST* syntax is useful on the borders (fulcrums) of the ROC abstraction. On the inside (for tools), I prefer *active* syntax.

The easiest way to accomplish this is to create a new nCoDE endpoint, *helloWorldActive*, based on our *helloWorld* endpoint (Figure 8-14).

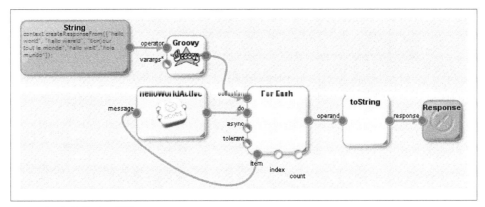

Figure 8-15. helloWorldTester

That looks a bit like a futile exercise, but here are the properties of the *helloWorldActive* endpoint.

name

helloWorldActive

id

chapter8:ncode:helloWorldActive

grammar

```
<grammar>
  <active>
    <identifier>active:helloworld</identifier>
    <argument name="message" min="1" max="1"/>
  </active>
</grammar>
```

So, now we have two ways to reach our *helloWorld* service. In the test battery, we will use the second way, but by all means fire up the Visualizer to prove to yourself that the same physical endpoint gets executed.

helloWorldTester

Composing a test battery is really trivial now (see Figure 8-15).

To be able to make this endpoint, you need to <u>add</u> the *following import* in the chapter 8 nCoDE rootspace.

```
<import>
  <uri>urn:org:netkernel:lang:groovy</uri>
  <private/>
</import>
```

Why is Groovy needed? Well, the *For Each* element requires a collection (list, array, and so on). None of the elements in the *Literals* palette provides that, so I get a collection from a small Groovy program.

Figure 8-16. helloWorld unittest result

Everything is a resource; the Groovy program itself is a *String* element. Here it is:

```
context.createResponseFrom(["hello world", "hallo wereld", "bonjour tout le
monde","hallo welt","hola mundo"]);
```

That is one mandatory argument of the *For Each* covered. The second one, *do*, might be somewhat less intuitive. Obviously, we want our *helloWorldActive* endpoint executed in each iteration. So, why do we link the output of that endpoint to the *do* argument?

The image may confuse you because you expect to read it from *left to right*. Actually, you need to read it from *right to left*:

1. A *response* from our endpoint is requested.
2. A *toString* accessor request is going to provide it.
3. It processes an iterable that is the result of a *For Each* accessor.
4. The collection to iterate over is provided by the *Groovy runtime*.
5. The do block is provided by the *helloWorldActive* endpoint.
6. The Groovy runtime needs an operator (program), which is provided as a *String*.
7. The *HelloWorldActive* endpoint needs a message, which is provided as an *item* from the collection.

Most mysteries should be resolved now, but there's still the *toString* accessor. Why is that there?

Because I'm lazy! It is the easiest way to turn the result of the *For Each* accessor (an iterable) into something readable by humans. What should be there is some postprocessing that takes the result and turns it—in this case—into a test battery report. I'll leave that as an exercise for you.

You can see the result in Figure 8-16.

Conclusion

nCoDE is not *just* a composition tool. The purpose for which a person uses it also defines that person's role in the IT organization![2]

2. Although many managers will not agree with me, this sentence does not have the cart before the horse.

PART III

Appendixes

Appendix: useless when quiet, in danger of removal when obtrusive . . .

Getting and Installing NetKernel

Most of us in IT (myself included) have the *I'll read the instructions later* approach. Well, here are the instructions.

Prerequisites

To run NetKernel, you must have a computer and operating system capable of running Java 6. NetKernel is platform neutral and has been deployed successfully on Windows 2000, Windows XP, Windows Vista, Windows Server 2003, Apple Mac OS X, Linux (Redhat, Suse, Debian, Ubuntu), and Solaris.

The above comes straight from the install notes. I just want to add that although a JRE (java runtime environment) is sufficient to run NetKernel with all its features, I strongly advise you to install a JDK (java development kit) on machines where you do NetKernel development.

Download

This book deals with the open source NetKernel Standard Edition (Figure A-1).

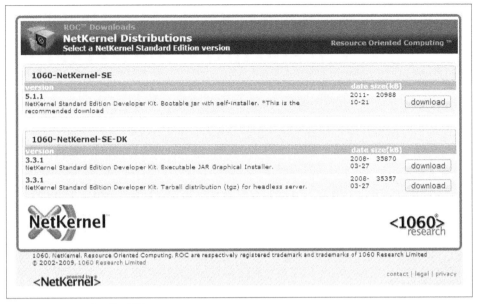

Figure A-1. Download NKSE

1. <u>Select</u> *the download button* for the 5.1.x. version.
2. <u>Select</u> *the download button* for the mirror nearest to you.
3. <u>Save</u> *the 1060-NetKernel-5.1.x.jar file* to your system.
4. While the download is running, <u>read</u> *the install notes*.

Installation

Installation is very easy and pretty much identical on any platform. Below, you'll find the transcripts of an installation on Windows 7 and Ubuntu 10.04 LTS—the Lucid Lynx.

Running the downloaded jar—Windows

1. <u>Position</u> yourself in *the directory* above the one where you want to install NetKernel (I'm going to install in D:\NK5, so I position in D:, I also put the downloaded jar there for ease of use).

2. <u>Start</u> *the downloaded jar*.

```
C:\Users\your_user>d:
D:\>java -jar 1060-NetKernel-SE-5.1.1.jar
Expanding urn.com.ten60.core.boot-1.18.22
Expanding urn.com.ten60.core.cache.se-1.5.11
Expanding urn.com.ten60.core.layer0-1.81.57
Expanding urn.com.ten60.core.module.standard-1.56.29
```

```
Expanding urn.com.ten60.core.netkernel.api-4.1.5
Expanding urn.com.ten60.core.netkernel.impl-4.23.24
I 18:29:15 Kernel
Starting 1060-NetKernel-SE
Resource Oriented Computing Platform
Version 5.1.1
Copyright 2002-2010 1060 Research Limited  http://www.1060research.com
1060, NetKernel, Resource Oriented Computing are Trademarks of 1060 Research Ltd
...
I 18:29:21 Kernel         NetKernel Ready, accepting requests...
I 18:29:21 ModuleManager System now at RunLevel [2]
*********************************************************************
* JAR BOOT NOTES
* --------------
* NetKernel is now running an HTTP server on port 1060
*
* To start using NetKernel open a web browser
* and go to:   http://localhost:1060/
*********************************************************************
```

Running the downloaded jar—Ubuntu

Starting the downloaded jar on Linux is exactly the same as on Windows, but we are
going to do a bit of preparation in advance. This will make things easier later on.

```
your_user@ubuntumachine:~$ sudo groupadd --gid 1060 dexter
your_user@ubuntumachine:~$ sudo useradd --uid 1060 --gid 1060 \
 -m -d /home/dexter -s /bin/bash -c 'NetKernel software' dexter
your_user@ubuntumachine:~$ sudo passwd dexter
your_user@ubuntumachine:~$ sudo mkdir /usr/NK5
your_user@ubuntumachine:~$ sudo chown dexter:dexter /usr/NK5
```

You can, of course, pick your own group name, username and directory names. The
rest of this installation procedure will go with the values used above.

```
dexter@ubuntumachine:~$ cd /usr
dexter@ubuntumachine:/usr$ java -jar /var/tmp/1060-NetKernel-SE-5.1.1.jar
Expanding urn.com.ten60.core.boot-1.18.22
Expanding urn.com.ten60.core.cache.se-1.5.11
Expanding urn.com.ten60.core.layer0-1.81.57
Expanding urn.com.ten60.core.module.standard-1.56.29
Expanding urn.com.ten60.core.netkernel.api-4.1.5
Expanding urn.com.ten60.core.netkernel.impl-4.23.24
I 18:29:15 Kernel
Starting 1060-NetKernel-SE
Resource Oriented Computing Platform
Version 5.1.1
Copyright 2002-2010 1060 Research Limited  http://www.1060research.com
1060, NetKernel, Resource Oriented Computing are Trademarks of 1060 Research Ltd
...
I 18:29:21 Kernel         NetKernel Ready, accepting requests...
I 18:29:21 ModuleManager System now at RunLevel [2]
*********************************************************************
* JAR BOOT NOTES
* --------------
```

Figure A-2. NetKernel management console

```
* NetKernel is now running an HTTP server on port 1060
*
* To start using NetKernel open a web browser
* and go to:   http://localhost:1060/
*******************************************************************
```

Verification—all environments

If all is well, you can now:

1. <u>Start</u> your *favorite web browser*.
2. <u>Browse</u> to *http://localhost:1060*.

 The NetKernel interface will perform well on any *modern, up-to-date* web browser.

You should get the *NetKernel management console* (Figure A-2) on what is called the NetKernel Backend HTTPFulcrum (more on that further on).

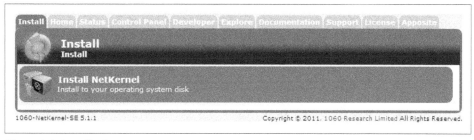

Figure A-3. Install tab

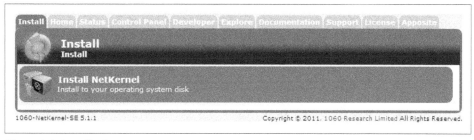

Figure A-4. Install to disk

Installation—all environments

By all means, browse through the tabs and check stuff (you probably did not read that *Readme First!*, did you?). When you're ready for the installation to disk, <u>select</u> the *Install* tab (Figure A-3).

Are you wondering too what the *Install NetKernel* option means? <u>Select</u> *it* to find out!

Read the license you'll see next. This book is concerned only with the *NetKernel Standard Edition*. If you cannot comply with the public license terms you must obtain a commercial license from 1060 Research (*http://www.1060research.com*). If you understand and agree with it, <u>accept</u> *the license*.

All the earlier housekeeping and positioning pays off here (see Figure A-4), for by <u>entering</u> *NK5* in the *Target Directory field*, the installation will go where we want it (as well on Windows as on Linux). <u>Select</u> *Install*.

Verification—Windows

The following message will show: *NetKernel was successfully installed onto your filesystem at D:\\NK5.*

Check visually that *five new subdirectories* have been created underneath D:\NK5.

```
D:\NK5>dir
  Volume in drive D is xxxx
  Volume Serial Number is xxxx-xxxx

  Directory of D:\NK5

04/09/2010 21:18 <DIR> .
04/09/2010 21:18 <DIR> ..
04/09/2010 21:18 <DIR> bin
04/09/2010 21:18 <DIR> etc
04/09/2010 21:18 <DIR> lib
04/09/2010 21:18 <DIR> log
04/09/2010 21:18 <DIR> modules
              0 File(s) 0 bytes
              7 Dir(s) x bytes free
```

Verification—Ubuntu

The following message will show : *NetKernel was successfully installed onto your file-system at /usr/NK5.*

Check visually that *five new subdirectories* have been created underneath /usr/NK5.

```
dexter@ubuntumachine:/usr/NK5$ ls -la
total 28
drwxr-xr-x  7 dexter dexter 4096 2010-09-04 21:16 .
drwxr-xr-x 14 root   root   4096 2010-09-04 17:20 ..
drwxr-xr-x  2 dexter dexter 4096 2010-09-04 21:16 bin
drwxr-xr-x  4 dexter dexter 4096 2010-09-04 21:16 etc
drwxr-xr-x  4 dexter dexter 4096 2010-09-04 21:16 lib
drwxr-xr-x  2 dexter dexter 4096 2010-09-04 21:16 log
drwxr-xr-x 36 dexter dexter 4096 2010-09-04 21:16 modules
```

Stopping downloaded jar - all environments

You are now almost ready for your first run. Follow *the instructions for shutdown* in your browser. This will gracefully stop the installation run.

```
I 20:55:27 Kernel         NetKernel Pausing, flushing pending requests, new requests
queued...
I 20:55:27 HTTPTranspor~ Decommissioning HTTP Transport
...
I 20:55:30 Kernel         NetKernel shutdown complete
```

First run from disk—Windows

Ready for your first run:

```
C:\Users\your_user>d:
D:\>cd NK5
D:\NK5>bin\netkernel.bat
I 21:02:43 Kernel
```

```
Starting 1060-NetKernel-SE
Resource Oriented Computing Platform
Version 5.1.1
Copyright 2002-2010 1060 Research Limited  http://www.1060research.com
1060, NetKernel, Resource Oriented Computing are Trademarks of 1060 Research Ltd.
...
I 21:03:24 HTTPTranspor~ Starting [HTTP] on port [1060]
I 21:03:24 Kernel       NetKernel Ready, accepting requests...
I 21:03:24 ModuleManager System now at RunLevel [7]
I 21:03:24 InitEndpoint  Init completed - system at RunLevel [7]
I 21:03:24 CronTransport Added Job [Apposite Synchronize @ Every 3rd Day] of type
[crontab]
I 21:03:25 ModuleListAc~ ModuleListAccessor complete
```

First run from disk—Ubuntu

Ready for your first run:

```
dexter@ubuntumachine:~$ cd /usr/NK5
dexter@ubuntumachine:~$ bin/netkernel.sh
I 21:02:43 Kernel
Starting 1060-NetKernel-SE
Resource Oriented Computing Platform
Version 5.1.1
Copyright 2002-2010 1060 Research Limited  http://www.1060research.com
1060, NetKernel, Resource Oriented Computing are Trademarks of 1060 Research Ltd.
...
I 21:03:24 HTTPTranspor~ Starting [HTTP] on port [1060]
I 21:03:24 Kernel       NetKernel Ready, accepting requests...
I 21:03:24 ModuleManager System now at RunLevel [7]
I 21:03:24 InitEndpoint  Init completed - system at RunLevel [7]
I 21:03:24 CronTransport Added Job [Apposite Synchronize @ Every 3rd Day] of type
[crontab]
I 21:03:25 ModuleListAc~ ModuleListAccessor complete
```

Verification - all environments

If all is well, you can now once again:

1. Start your *favorite web browser*
2. Browse to *http://localhost:1060*.

The only visible difference between this *NetKernel management console* (Figure A-5) and the one we saw earlier (Figure A-2) is that the *Install* tab is no longer there.

Apposite—all environments

Before you do anything else, you should update the current NetKernel modules to make sure you have all security and other patches. NetKernel has a Software Management System called *Apposite* to take care of this. In fact, Apposite itself is managed and updated this way, as is every part of NetKernel.

Figure A-5. NetKernel management onsole

The default location (Base URI) where Apposite finds its updates is the online Apposite Repository (*http://apposite.netkernel.org/repo/*). If your NetKernel instance does not have access to the Internet, you'll not be able to reach this. In that case, you should *first* set up your own. Appendix B explains how to do this. Only then continue with the remainder of this appendix.

Select *the Apposite tab* of the NetKernel management console.

Select the *Apposite Software Management System*.

You should have seen *orange* on the selection screen (Figure A-6), and you should see *orange* here (Figure A-7)! There should be updates available. If there are no updates available at this point, something went wrong in an earlier step. [1] The action to take next suggests itself rather clearly: select the *Select All Updates* button.

---

1. You might be working with a recent release for which no updates are available yet. This is not impossible, just unlikely. Check!

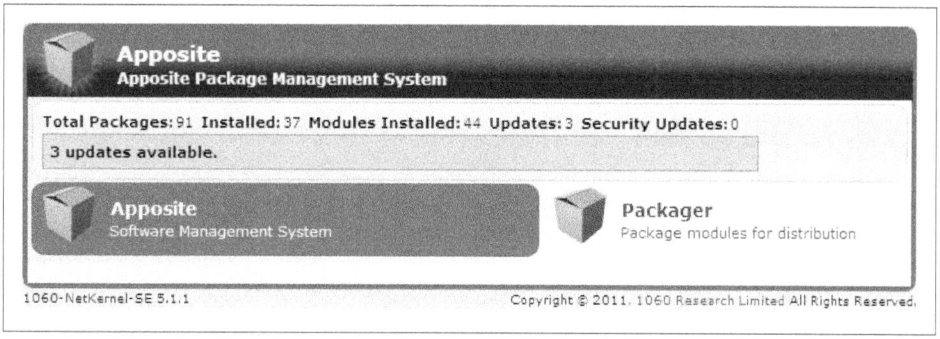

Figure A-6. Apposite tab

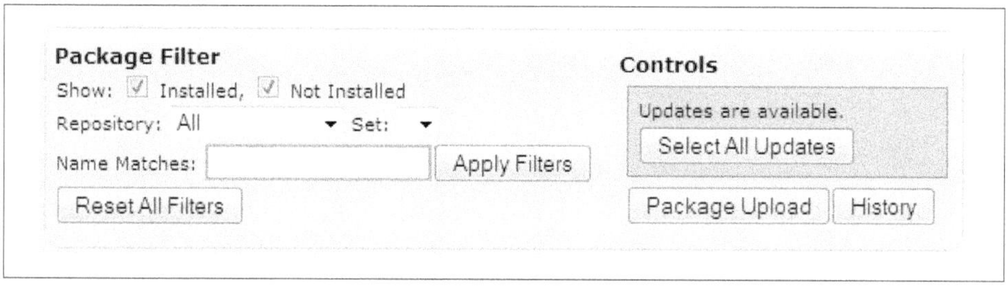

Figure A-7. Updates available

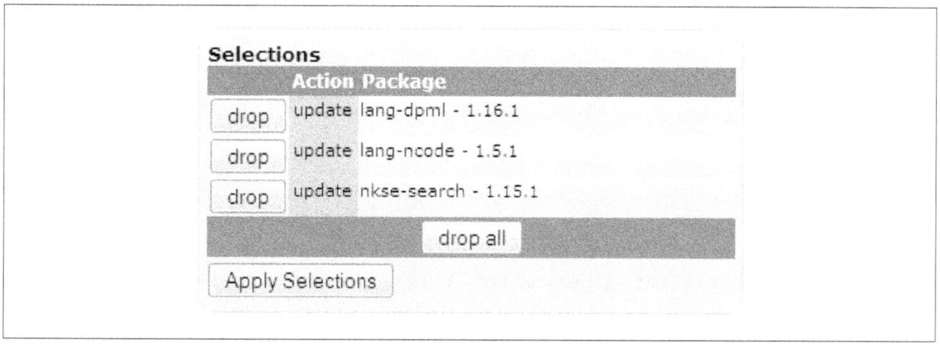

Figure A-8. Selections

A *Selections* list (Figure A-8) will appear on the right-hand side. I do know that you immediately want to add other stuff (Python, for example) as well, but *don't!* Take the logical next step, and <u>select</u> the *Apply Selections* button.

Be patient, depending on which repository you use this may take a minute or so. Underneath the *Selections* list you'll get an update of what's going on. A *Refresh* button will appear when the updates have been applied.

Guess what you have to do next? That's right: <u>select</u> the *Refresh* button. If all goes well, you should get the Apposite screen back, with all updated packages showing their new version number and all *orange* gone!

Conclusion

Installing NetKernel is—considering what you get in return—pretty simple and uniform across platforms. For a production system, you might want to run NetKernel as a service or a daemon that gets started at boot time. Appendix C deals with setting that up.

Setting Up Your Own Apposite Repository

Every IT environment has different needs and requirements. Having your own copy of the main Apposite Repository may go a long way in making NetKernel comply with them. This chapter explains how to set up that copy.

Prerequisites

There is a bit of a "chicken and the egg" problem[1] here. The reason you would need your own Apposite Repository is that you do not or will not allow your NetKernel instance access to the Internet. However, in order to set up your own Apposite Repository, you will need access to the Internet. There's no way around it, I'm afraid. It does not, however, have to be from the machine you run your NetKernel instance on!

I'll discuss a setup via the *rsync* utility on Windows 7 and Ubuntu 10.04 LTS—the Lucid Lynx. For Ubuntu, this utility is present by default, but for Windows 7, we'll use the one available in the *Cygwin* package. Don't worry if Cygwin means nothing to you. I'll discuss the setup for that as well. In fact, that's what I'm going to do first.

 Yes, I do know that there are other rsync ports available for Windows. Feel free to use them, but most of them are not (free to use, that is). Some of the others are limited to specific usages. Trust me, it will do you no harm to have a Linux-like shell with lots of Linux utilities available on your Windows machine. You can thank me later!

Preparation

Preparation is half the job!

---

1. That one has been solved by science: the chicken came first. It's something to do with a certain protein.

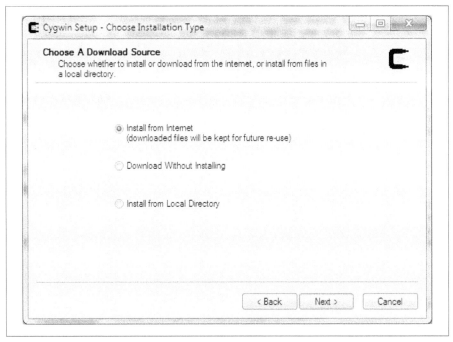

Figure B-1. Setup—Install from Internet

Getting Cygwin—Windows

Download the *Cygwin setup file (http://cygwin.com/)*. Note that not only the first install is done with this file, but also all subsequent updates (or installation of new utilities you may require). So download it to a place where you can find it again (a link on your desktop may come in handy).

Installing Cygwin—Windows

1. Start the downloaded *setup.exe*.
2. Read *the text* (told you about keeping the *setup.exe* file, didn't I?).
3. Select *Next* (Figure B-1).
4. Select *Install from Internet*.
5. Select *Next* (Figure B-2).
6. Enter *the location* and *the users*.
7. Select *Next* (Figure B-3).
8. Enter *the location* to which you want Cygwin to download its packages.
9. Select *Next* (Figure B-4).

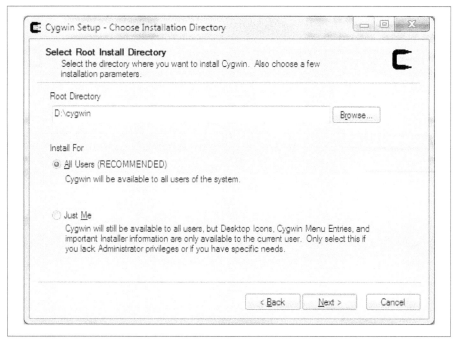

Figure B-2. Setup—Location

10. <u>Select</u> *your connection type* (for me, its *Direct Connection* at home and *Internet Explorer Proxy Settings* at work).

11. <u>Select</u> *Next*.

12. <u>Select</u> *a mirror* near you.

13. <u>Select</u> *Next* (Figure B-6).

14. Finally, we are getting to the packages (Linux utilities) that are going to be installed. For the most part, the defaults are fine, but there are *three packages* that you want to <u>select</u> (in order to select a package, expand the heading and click on the skip in front of the package name; the skip will be replaced by a version number):

```
openssh (Net)
rsync (Net)
subversion (Devel)
```

15. <u>Select</u> *Next*.

16. <u>Confirm</u> *the installation* of packages resolving dependencies.

17. <u>Select</u> *Next*.

18. The installation will now run for a bit (Figure B-7).

19. <u>Select</u> *the icons* you want to create.

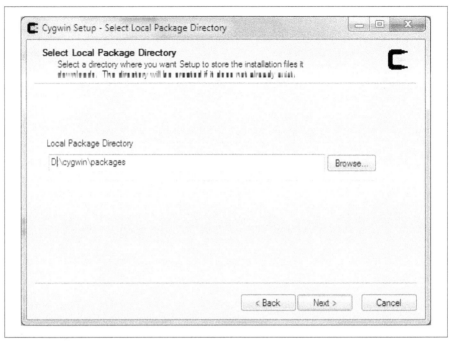

Figure B-3. Setup—Download location

20. Select *Finish*.

Congratulations! You are now the proud owner of a quite decent Linux environment on your Windows machine.

Nonroot user—Ubuntu

If the Linux machine for the Apposite Repository differs from the NetKernel machine, you will benefit from creating the same non-root user we created for the NetKernel machine.

```
your_user@ubuntumachine:~$ sudo groupadd --gid 1060 dexter
your_user@ubuntumachine:~$ sudo useradd --uid 1060 --gid 1060 \
 -m -d /home/dexter -s /bin/bash -c 'Apposite Repository' dexter
your_user@ubuntumachine:~$ sudo passwd dexter
```

Synchronization

Her'es how to get the copy and keep it up to date!

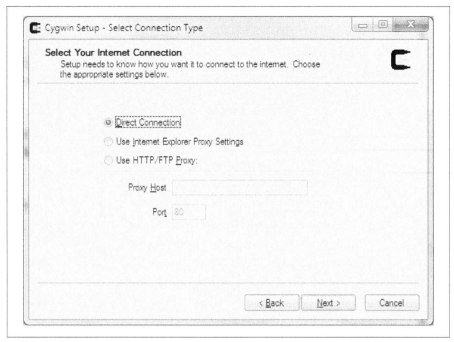

Figure B-4. Setup—Connection type

Creating the repository—Windows

Create a directory to hold the repository.

```
C:\Users\your_user>mkdir d:\repo
```

Creating the repository—Ubuntu

Create a directory to hold the repository.

```
your_user@ubuntumachine:~$ sudo mkdir /repo
your_user@ubuntumachine:~$ sudo chown dexter:dexter /repo
```

Synchronizing the repository—Windows

Start your Cygwin shell (double-click the icon that was created on your desktop). Then execute the following command to take care of the synchronization itself.

```
your_user@windowshost ~$ rsync -rv \
  rsync://apposite.netkernel.org/download/repo/ /cygdrive/d/repo/
```

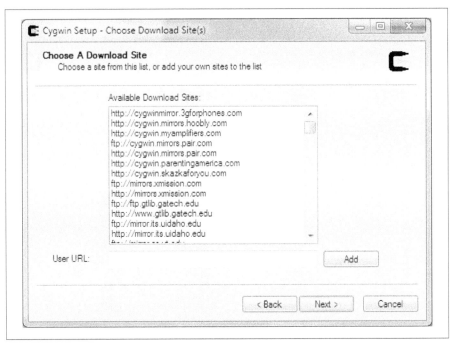

Figure B-5. Setup—Mirror

 If you are using a firewall (you should), it will ask you if rsync is allowed access to the Internet. Grant that access. A second later, it will come back to ask if rsync may act as a server. It may.

The synchronization will take a while. The repository at the time of download (which was August 2011) was about 375 Mb.

Synchronizing the repository—Ubuntu

Log on *to the system* as the nonroot user we created earlier.

```
dexter@ubuntumachine:~$ rsync -rv \
    rsync://apposite.netkernel.org/download/repo/ /repo/
```

The synchronization will take a while. The repository at the time of download (which was August 2011) was about 375 Mb.

Verification—Windows

You should see two directories in the repository.

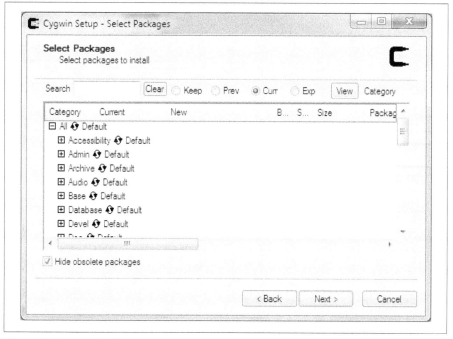

Figure B-6. Setup—Packages

```
C:\Users\your_user>dir d:\repo
 Volume in drive D is xxxx
 Volume Serial Number is xxxx-xxxx

 Directory of d:\repo

09/09/2010  21:17    <DIR>          .
09/09/2010  21:17    <DIR>          ..
09/09/2010  21:17    <DIR>          netkernel
09/09/2010  21:17    <DIR>          packages
               0 File(s) 0 bytes
               4 Dir(s) x bytes free
```

Verification—Ubuntu

You should see two directories in the repository.

```
dexter@ubuntumachine:~$ ls -la /repo
total 16
drwxr-xr-x  4 dexter dexter 4096 2010-09-09 21:31 .
drwxr-xr-x 23 root   root   4096 2010-09-09 21:06 ..
drwxr-xr-x  3 dexter dexter 4096 2010-09-09 21:31 netkernel
drwxr-xr-x 38 dexter dexter 4096 2010-09-09 21:31 packages
```

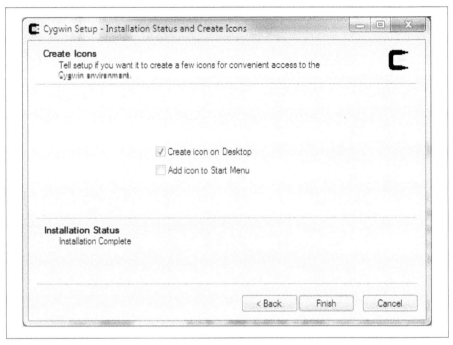

Figure B-7. Setup—Icons

Use

There are several ways you can go about this. You can *serve* the Apposite Repository to the NetKernel instance(s) through a web server. In Chapter 3, there's a section on how to use NetKernel as a web server.

Another option is to *map* the Apposite Repository over your internal network to the NetKernel instance(s). Windows has several options for just that, and with *Samba* you can easily map a Linux directory to a Windows machine (the other way around remains a tricky thing, though).

For the rest of this Appendix, I assume that you have *manually copied* the Apposite Repository to the machine that is running the NetKernel instance. Whatever option you take, remember to frequently resynchronize with the central repository on the Internet! Once a month, for example, will not hurt at all.

 Automate this task or have it automated. It is all very well to be closed off from the *evil* Internet, and no, you do not always need the latest and greatest, but you do need security patches and the occasional new functionality. If you have to do it manually, you'll forget after a while.

Activating your personal Apposite Repository—Windows

These are my assumptions:

- You are <u>running</u> the *NetKernel instance* on this machine.
- You <u>copied</u> the *synchronized Apposite Repository* to this machine; in my case, that is to **D:\repo**.

These are the necessary actions :

1. <u>Navigate</u> to the *NetKernel Apposite screen* (http://localhost:1060 and so on, remember?).
2. <u>Select</u> the *Admin button*.
3. <u>Change</u> the *Admin Base URI* of the repository (Figure B-8).

   ```
   from http://apposite.netkernel.org/repo/
   to   file:///D:/repo/
   ```

4. <u>Test</u> the *three connections* to verify they are working correctly.

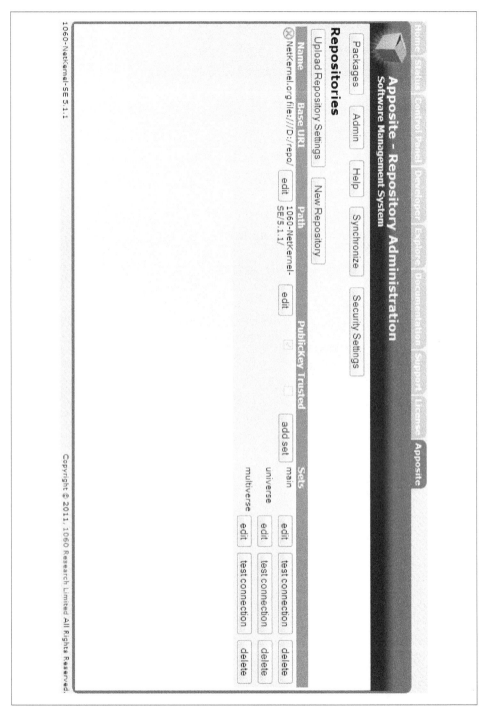

Figure B-8. Repositories

Activating your personal Apposite Repository—Ubuntu

These are my assumptions:

- You are <u>running</u> the *NetKernel instance* on this machine.
- You <u>copied</u> the *synchronized Apposite Repository* to this machine; in my case, that is to **/repo**.

These are the necessary actions:

1. <u>Navigate</u> to the *NetKernel Apposite screen* (http://localhost:1060 and so on, re-member?).
2. <u>Select</u> the *Admin button*.
3. <u>Change</u> the *Admin Base URI* of the repository (Figure B-9).

   ```
   from http://apposite.netkernel.org/repo/
   to   file:/repo/
   ```

4. Test the three connections to verify they are working correctly.

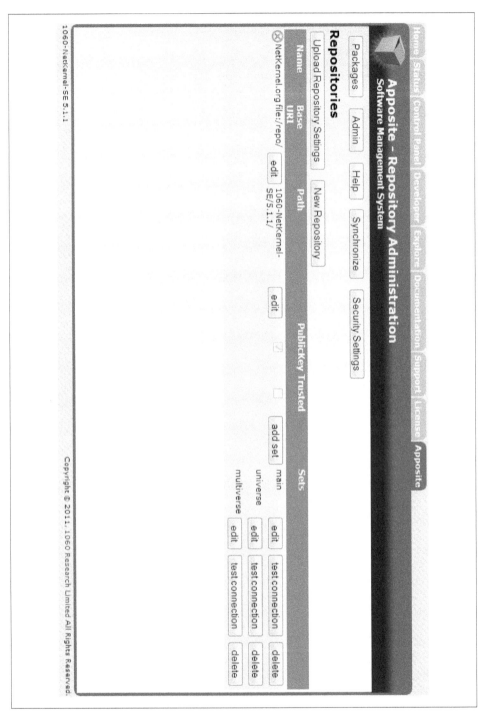

Figure B-9. Repositories

Conclusion

Setting up your own *Apposite Repository* is not hard at all. I would even dare to say it is an advisable thing to do for the following reasons:

- Your security team—if you have one—will be pleased.
- If you have to comply with change-procedures/change-windows, you can.
- If you have multiple NetKernel instances running, your updates will be much swifter from a local (local as in *on your local network*) repository.

However, I would also advise to do the following:

- Automate the synchronization with the official repository.
- Update your instances frequently.

Running NetKernel as a Service

Doing stuff as a service is very hot these days. I, for one, do not have my head in the clouds. You'll find some decent information about *Naas* (note the lowercase s) in this appendix.

Cover Story

For servers, the following is expected behaviour, but imagine this: *You get up in the morning, boot your home desktop or laptop[1] and NetKernel is automatically started.* Bliss!

As you probably know, attaining the state of bliss is not one of the lighter matters. However, Peter Rodgers has provided all that you require to run NetKernel as a service (on your server or on your home desktop) in the NetKernel forums.

If you feel comfortable with the instructions mentioned in that post, by all means follow them and ignore the rest of this Appendix. There's going to be slightly more detail in the procedure below. There are also going to be platform-specific instructions.

 I only vouch for the platforms on which I tested the procedures. At this time, those are Windows 7 and Ubuntu 10.04 LTS—the Lucid Lynx. That means they will probably work on most current Windows platforms and Linux platforms.

Procedure Windows 7

Creating your own service on Windows is not one of the lighter matters. Here is the walk-through.

---

1. If this is indeed the first thing you do in the morning (as it is for me), get a life, and let me know where you found one.

Download Java Service Wrapper

Being raised on Linux, I find this ridiculous. When I want something started at boot time, a simple script and a couple of links do the trick. Basic functionality, no? It isn't, not on Windows. I searched high and low for a supported way to turn the *netkernel.bat* script into a service that I could start/stop/restart like any service. While I found some really interesting stuff—you have to take a look at *Autoruns* and the other SysInternals—there is simply nothing but ugly hacks.

Since *netkernel.bat* starts a Java process, there is another solution. Enter the Tanuki Java service wrapper. We will lose some flexibility, but it is excellent software, and the community version suits us fine.

But wait . . . no 64-bit version available? No problem; with the source available, somebody was bound to create a 64-bit version.

Download the *version* that suits your Windows environment.

- wrapper-windows-x86-32-3.5.13
- wrapper-windows-x86-64-3.5.7

Unpack the *zipfile* in a location that suits you. We are not going to run directly from there, so it doesn't really matter. I'll refer to that location further on as *[jswlocation]*.

Install Java Service Wrapper

In a first step, we are going to copy the relevant files from *[jswlocation]* to *[install]* (the directory where NetKernel is installed).

- *wrapper.exe* from *[jswlocation]/bin* to *[install]/bin*
- *InstallTestWrapper-NT.bat* from *[jswlocation]/bin* to *[install]/bin/InstallNetKernel-NT.bat*
- *UnInstallTestWrapper-NT.bat* from *[jswlocation]/bin* to *[install]/bin/UnInstallNetKernel-NT.bat*
- *wrapper.dll* from *[jswlocation]/lib* to *[install]/bin*
- *wrapper.jar* from *[jswlocation]/lib* to *[install]/lib*

The second step is to alter the *[install]/bin/*InstallNetkernel-NT.bat* scripts. The *_WRAPPER_CONF_DEFAULT* line in both files must look like this:

```
set _WRAPPER_CONF_DEFAULT=../etc/netkernel_jsw.conf
```

The third and final step is to create the *[install]/etc/netkernel_jsw.conf* file.

```
#encoding=UTF-8

wrapper.lang=en_US

set.NETKERNEL_HOME=D:\NK5
```

```
set.JAVA_HOME=C:\Program Files\Java\jdk1.6.0_27

wrapper.java.command=%JAVA_HOME%\bin\java
wrapper.java.mainclass=org.tanukisoftware.wrapper.WrapperSimpleApp
wrapper.java.classpath.1=..\lib\urn.com.ten60.core.boot-1.18.22.jar
wrapper.java.classpath.2=..\lib\wrapper.jar
wrapper.java.library.path.1=.
wrapper.java.additional.auto_bits=TRUE
wrapper.java.additional.1=-XX:SoftRefLRUPolicyMSPerMB=100
wrapper.java.additional.2=-Dfile.encoding=UTF-8
wrapper.java.additional.3=-Djava.endorsed.dirs=D:\NK5\lib\endorsed
wrapper.java.additional.4=-
Djava.protocol.handler.pkgs=org.ten60.netkernel.protocolhandler
wrapper.java.additional.5=-Dsun.net.client.defaultConnectTimeout=20000
wrapper.java.additional.6=-Dsun.net.client.defaultReadTimeout=20000
wrapper.java.additional.7=-Xmx128m
wrapper.java.initmemory=128
wrapper.java.maxmemory=128

wrapper.app.parameter.1=BootLoader
wrapper.app.parameter.2=D:\NK5

wrapper.console.format=PM
wrapper.console.loglevel=INFO

wrapper.logfile=..\log\wrapper.log
wrapper.logfile.format=LPTM
wrapper.logfile.loglevel=INFO
wrapper.logfile.maxsize=50000000
wrapper.logfile.maxfiles=3

wrapper.syslog.loglevel=NONE

wrapper.ignore_sequence_gaps=TRUE

wrapper.console.title=NetKernel

wrapper.check.deadlock=TRUE
wrapper.check.deadlock.interval=10
wrapper.max_failed_invocations=99
wrapper.console.fatal_to_stderr=FALSE
wrapper.console.error_to_stderr=FALSE
wrapper.check.deadlock.action=RESTART
wrapper.check.deadlock.output=FULL
wrapper.filter.trigger.1000=java.lang.OutOfMemoryError
wrapper.filter.action.1000=RESTART
wrapper.filter.message.1000=The JVM has run out of memory.

wrapper.name=NetKernel
wrapper.displayname=NetKernel
wrapper.description=NetKernel Service
wrapper.ntservice.dependency.1=
wrapper.ntservice.starttype=AUTO_START
wrapper.ntservice.interactive=false
```

The above contents are based on the templates in *[jswlocation]/conf*. Note the use of the *WrapperSimpleApp*, a helper class that provides service control elements. Our own class is passed as a parameter to it. Also note that the console output can be found in *[install]/log/wrapper.log*.

The flexibility we lose is, well, everything is hardcoded in the configuration. Next time the NetKernel boot jar changes, we'll have to change this configuration manually.

Activate NetKernel service

Activating the service is easy:

```
cd [install]/bin
InstallNetKernel-NT.bat
```

 You will need administrator privileges to do the above.

The NetKernel service will be started during the next reboot. If you want it started right now, you have to do that manually (Figure C-1).

Deactivate NetKernel service

Deactivating the service (if you would ever wish to do so) is easy. Stop the service first and then do the following:

```
cd [install]/bin
UnInstallNetKernel-NT.bat
```

 You will need administrator privileges to do the above.

Procedure Ubuntu 10.04

We could do the same, use the Tanuki wrapper, that is. By all means, do so if you feel so inclined, but I'm going to do it natively.

The netkerneld script

What follows is the longest piece of code in this book. It is a refresh of the netkerneld script that comes in the installation jar (in the bin directory).

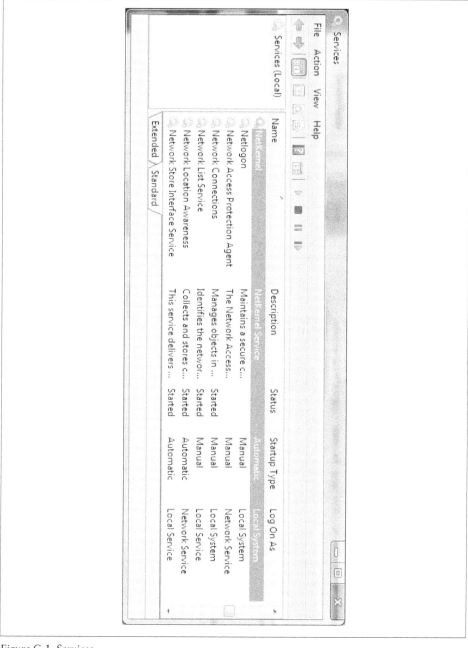

Figure C-1. Services

A jar file is basically just a zip, and if you change the extension to zip, most unzip tools will happily extract the files from it.

```bash
#!/bin/bash
# chkconfig.    82 18
# description: 1060 NetKernel

HOMEDIR=/usr/NK5
USER=dexter
APPNAME=NetKernel

# User Editable variables
GREPPID="ten60.pid=1" # Must match the ten60.pid value set
                      # in the netkernel.sh script
BACKEND="1060"        # HTTP port of backend fulcrum

# Local variables
INITSCRIPT=$HOMEDIR/bin/netkernel.sh
STOPURL="http://localhost:$BACKEND/tools/shutdown?action2=force"
REBOOTURL="http://localhost:$BACKEND/tools/reboot?action2=force"
POLLURL="http://localhost:$BACKEND"
GREPTEXT="BootLoader"

# Logging Path - add this to your logrotate schedule as required
LOGFILE="$HOMEDIR/log/netkernel.out"

# Check for init script
if [ ! -f $INITSCRIPT ]; then
  echo "$APPNAME not available... (no  $INITSCRIPT)" >&2
  exit 1
fi

# Check user identity
ID=$(id -u "$USER" 2>/dev/null)
if [ -z "$ID" ]; then
  echo "$USER is not a user. Please create a account first" >&2
  echo "This script controls NetKernel as a daemon" >&2
  echo "you can start NetKernel directly with netkernel.sh" >&2
  exit 1
fi

setpslist() {
  pslist=$(ps ax --width=2000 | \
    grep "$GREPTEXT" | \
    grep "$GREPPID" | \
    grep -v PID | \
    awk '{printf $1 " "}')
}

start() {
  setpslist

  if [ ! -z "$pslist" ]; then
    echo "$APPNAME already running, can't start it" >&2
```

```
    return 1
  fi

  echo -n "Starting $APPNAME: "

  if [ ! -e "$LOGFILE" ]; then
     touch $LOGFILE
     chown $USER:$USER $LOGFILE
  fi

  exec su - -p --shell=/bin/sh $USER \
    -c "$INITSCRIPT &>\"$LOGFILE\"" &>"$LOGFILE" &

  local starttime=$(date +"%s")

  while true; do
    sleep 3
    local now=$(date +"%s")

    if wget --tries=1 --timeout=1 \
       --server-response -O - "$POLLURL" 2>&1 | \
       grep -qai " HTTP/1.1 "; then
       echo "Started"
       break
    fi

    if [ $(($now - 10)) -gt $starttime ]; then
       setpslist
       if [ -z "$pslist" ]; then
         echo "Java not starting up, $APPNAME not running.">&2
         tail -10 $LOGFILE
         return 1
       fi
    fi

    if [ $(($now - 50)) -gt $starttime ]; then
       echo "Startup taking too long, giving up" >&2;
       return 1
    fi

    echo -n .
  done
}

stop() {
  setpslist

  if [ -z "$pslist" ]; then
    echo "$APPNAME not running, no need to stop it"
    return 0
  fi

  echo -n "Shutting down $APPNAME: "

  wget --tries=1 --timeout=1 \
```

```
      --server-response -O - $STOPURL 2>&1 | \
     grep -qai " HTTP/1.1 "

  local needtokill=N
  local starttime=$(date +"%s")
  while true; do
    sleep 3
    local now=$(date +"%s")

    setpslist

    if [ -z "$pslist" ]; then
      echo "  Stopped"
      return 0
    fi

    if [ "$needtokill" = "Y" ]; then
      echo -n "  Killing. "
      kill -SIGKILL $pslist
    else
      if [ $(($now - 50)) -gt $starttime ]; then
        echo -n " graceful shutdown taking too long.";
        kill -SIGTERM $pslist
        needtokill=Y
      fi
    fi
    echo -n .
  done
}

status() {
  setpslist
  if [ ! -z "$pslist" ]; then
    echo -n "$APPNAME ( PIDs $pslist ) is running."

    if wget --tries=1 --timeout=1 \
      --server-response -O - "$POLLURL" 2>&1 | \
      grep -qai " HTTP/1.1 "; then
      echo " And listening on port $BACKEND."
    else
      echo " But not responding on port $BACKEND."
    fi
  else
    echo "$APPNAME is stopped"
  fi
}

case "$1" in
  start)
    start
    ;;
  stop)
    stop
    ;;
  restart)
```

```
      stop
      sleep 3
      start
      ;;
   status)
      status
      ;;
   *)
      echo "Usage: $0 {start|stop|reboot|status}"
      exit 1
esac

exit $?
```

I removed unneeded and obsolete options and code, reformatted it so it fits the book better, and so on.

Installing the netkerneld script

 You need administrator privileges to do this.

Place the *netkerneld script* in the */etc/init.d* directory, and provide it with the correct permissions:

```
sudo chown root:root /etc/init.d/netkerneld
sudo chmod 755 /etc/init.d/netkerneld
```

You can verify that you it installed correctly:

```
sudo service netkerneld status
NetKernel is stopped
```

Activating the netkerneld script

 You need administrator privileges to do this.

Symbolic links to the script determine in which runlevels it is started or stopped.

```
sudo update-rc.d netkerneld defaults 82 18
update-rc.d: warning: /etc/init.d/netkerneld missing LSB information
update-rc.d: see <http://wiki.debian.org/LSBInitScripts>
 Adding system startup for /etc/init.d/netkerneld ...
   /etc/rc0.d/K18netkerneld -> ../init.d/netkerneld
   /etc/rc1.d/K18netkerneld -> ../init.d/netkerneld
```

```
/etc/rc6.d/K18netkerneld -> ../init.d/netkerneld
/etc/rc2.d/S82netkerneld -> ../init.d/netkerneld
/etc/rc3.d/S82netkerneld -> ../init.d/netkerneld
/etc/rc4.d/S82netkerneld -> ../init.d/netkerneld
/etc/rc5.d/S82netkerneld -> ../init.d/netkerneld
```

The NetKernel service will be started during the next reboot. If you want it started right now, you have to do that manually.

Deactivating the netkerneld script

 You need administrator privileges to do this.

<u>Make</u> *sure* you've stopped the service first.

```
sudo update-rc.d -f netkerneld remove
 Removing any system startup links for /etc/init.d/netkerneld ...
   /etc/rc0.d/K18netkerneld
   /etc/rc1.d/K18netkerneld
   /etc/rc2.d/S82netkerneld
   /etc/rc3.d/S82netkerneld
   /etc/rc4.d/S82netkerneld
   /etc/rc5.d/S82netkerneld
   /etc/rc6.d/K18netkerneld
```

Deinstalling the netkerneld script

 You need administrator privileges to do this.

<u>Make</u> *sure* you've stopped and deactivated the service first.

```
sudo rm -f /etc/init.d/netkerneld
```

Alternative script

There are as many ways of doing startup scripts as there are Linux flavors. Check with your friendly Linux system administrator to see what has to be done for your system. The script will probably work for all of them.

Quid Pro Quo

While you've now gained control over the NetKernel service, this also means you are now bound by the regular control tools. Using the Backend HTTPFulcrum tools to shut down and reboot NetKernel is no longer allowed!

Locking Down Your NetKernel Instance

Originally, this appendix was Linux only and based on a how-to I once wrote for the NetKernel forum. In the meantime, I was able to experiment a bit with some Windows instances, and I'm happy that I can now also present a procedure for that platform.

Cover Story

These days, having your own (virtual) server on the Internet is within the reach of many. There is power in being able to show the world what you can do. However, with (great) power comes (great) responsibility. While no single server can withstand a coordinated attack, there is no need to hand over your paid-for server to the first script-kiddie that comes along, either.

As I said, client and server in what follows can be either Linux (tested with Ubuntu 10.04 LTS—the Lucid Lynx) or Windows (tested with Windows 7 Home Premium). Here's an overview of the components we will use:

Firewall
    For Linux, we will use iptables; for Windows, the default Windows Firewall.
SSH Client
    Both platforms will use openssh (*http://openssh.com/*); for Windows, that means openssh under Cygwin (*http://cygwin.com/*).
SSH Server
    Both platforms will use openssh; for Windows, that means openssh under Cygwin.

These are the points we want to accomplish:

1. Default remote access to the server: none. One non-standard port is opened for ssh access.
2. The Frontend HTTPFulcrum is remotely reachable (port 8080).
3. The Backend HTTPFulcrum is not remotely reachable (port 1060), but it can be tunneled to through the port opened for ssh.

Figure D-1. Desktop icons

 This is a very strict setup. My host provider allows it, but yours may not. My host only runs NetKernel; yours may run other stuff (requiring other ports) too.

Procedure Windows 7

In Appendix B, I explain how to install Cygwin and even how to get the *openssh* package. So, I'm not going to repeat that here. Install the *vim* package while you're at it, though.

Client

You're all done. You require nothing else. The tunneling to port 1060 on the server is explained further down.

Server

Before we get into the gritty details, you need to put a link to two administrative tools on your desktop; *Services* and *Windows Firewall with Advanced Security* (Figure D-1).

There. As you experiment, you'll need both of those quite often.

The Windows Firewall offers a good starting position. Every inbound port that is not strictly needed for a software is closed. Good.

That allows us to immediately move on to the second step, the setup of the ssh server (sshd). Right-select the *Cygwin Terminal icon*, and select *Run as administrator*.

Run the *ssh-host-config script*.

```
$ ssh-host-config -y

*** Query: Overwrite existing /etc/ssh_config file? (yes/no) yes
*** Info: Creating default /etc/ssh_config file
*** Query: Overwrite existing /etc/sshd_config file? (yes/no) yes
*** Info: Creating default /etc/sshd_config file

...
```

```
*** Info: This script plans to use 'cyg_server'.
*** Info: 'cyg_server' will only be used by registered services.
*** Query: Create new privileged user account 'cyg_server'? (yes/no) yes
*** Info: Please enter a password for new user cyg_server.  Please be sure
*** Info: that this password matches the password rules given on your system.
*** Info: Entering no password will exit the configuration.
*** Query: Please enter the password:
*** Query: Reenter:

*** Info: User 'cyg_server' has been created with password '********'.

...

*** Info: The sshd service has been installed under the 'cyg_server'
*** Info: account.  To start the service now, call "net start sshd" or
*** Info: "cygrunsrv -S sshd".  Otherwise, it will start automatically
*** Info: after the next reboot.

*** Info: Host configuration finished. Have fun!
```

The script pretty much runs itself (-y argument helps with that). You are only required to enter a password for the user that will run the ssh server. After the run, you should find a new service (see Figure D-2).

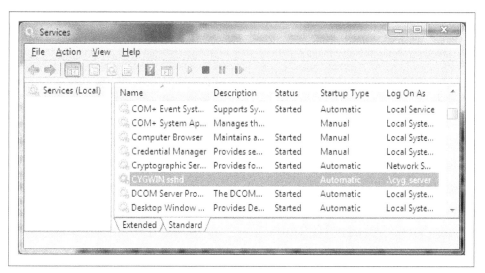

Figure D-2. New service

Don't start the service just yet. You need to edit the *sshd_config* file first.

```
$ vi /etc/sshd_config
```

Change the *port number* to something else. For this book, I'll go with 3022.

```
Port 3022
```

Security through obscurity may sound silly, but it works. Also, the port number I chose is outside the *normal* range of used ports. Only a patient scanner will bother with port numbers above 1000. The second thing to change is the *PermitTunnel* option. Uncomment *it*, and change *it* to yes.

```
PermitTunnel yes
```

Now you can start the *service*. Be sure to check *it* from another machine.

```
$ ssh -p 3022 youruser@yourhost
ssh: connect to host yourhost port 3022: Connection timed out
```

Did we forget something?

Firewall

Yes, we forgot something. I said the Windows Firewall offers a good starting position. Inbound port 3022 is neatly blocked. Time to start the *Windows Firewall with Advanced Security* (Figure D-3).

Perform the *following actions* to allow access on port 3022:

1. Select the *inbound rules.*
2. Select the *New Rule* option.
3. Set the *ruletype* to *port.* Select *Next.*
4. Set *specific local ports* to *3022.* TCP is fine. Select *Next.*
5. Set *action* to *Allow the connection.* Select *Next.*
6. Apply in *Domain, Private and Public.* Select *Next.*
7. Set *name* to *ssh inbound port.* Select *Finish.*
8. Check *it* again from another host.

```
$ ssh -p 3022 youruser@yourhost
youruser@yourhost ~$
```

That's better!

Procedure Ubuntu 10.04

SSH comes native on a Linux system. Make sure to verify, though!

Client

Check whether the *openssh-client package* is installed.

```
youruser@yourhost:~$ dpkg --get-selections openssh-client
openssh-client          install
```

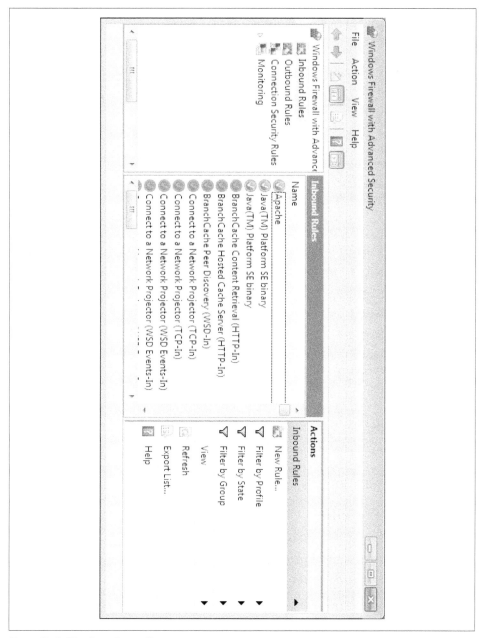

Figure D-3. Windows Firewall

If the same command on your system did not return the openssh-client line, you need to install the *openssh-client package.*

```
youruser@yourhost:~$ sudo apt-get install openssh-client
```

If you're not on Debian/Ubuntu, substitute with the package and package manager for your distribution.

You're all done. You require nothing else. The tunneling to port 1060 on the server is explained further down.

Server

<u>Check</u> whether the *openssh-server package* is installed.

```
youruser@yourhost:~$ dpkg --get-selections openssh-server
openssh-server          install
```

If the same command on your system did not return the openssh-server line, you need to <u>install</u> the *openssh-server package*.

```
youruser@yourhost:~$ sudo apt-get install openssh-server
```

Next, we <u>stop</u> the *sshd daemon*.

```
youruser@yourhost:~$ sudo service ssh stop
```

On most of the other Linux distributions, the service will be called sshd instead of ssh.

Edit the *sshd_config* file.

```
$ sudo vi /etc/ssh/sshd_config
```

<u>Change</u> the *port number* to something else. For this book I'll go with 3022.

```
Port 3022
```

Now you can <u>start</u> the *service*.

```
youruser@yourhost:~$ sudo service ssh start
```

<u>Check</u> *ssh access* from another machine.

```
$ ssh -p 3022 youruser@yourhost
youruser@yourhost's password:
Linux yourhost 2.6.32-36-generic #79-Ubuntu SMP Tue Nov 8 22:29:53 UTC 2011 x86_64 GNU/
Linux
Ubuntu 10.04.3 LTS

Welcome to Ubuntu!
 * Documentation:  https://help.ubuntu.com/

youruser@yourhost:~$
```

Firewall

Check if the *iptables package* is installed.

```
youruser@yourhost:~$ dpkg --get-selections iptables
iptables                install
```

If the same command on your system did not return the iptables line, you need to install the *iptables package*.

```
youruser@yourhost:~$ sudo apt-get install iptables
```

Next, we configure the *firewall*:

```
SERVER_IP=<your fixed SERVER ip>
sudo iptables -F
sudo iptables -X
sudo iptables -P INPUT DROP
sudo iptables -P OUTPUT DROP
sudo iptables -P FORWARD DROP
sudo iptables -A INPUT -i lo -j ACCEPT
sudo iptables -A OUTPUT -o lo -j ACCEPT
# In the next line replace 3022 with your choice for the SSH port
sudo iptables -A INPUT -p tcp -s 0/0 -d $SERVER_IP \
  --sport 513:65535 \
  --dport 3022 -m state \
  --state NEW,ESTABLISHED -j ACCEPT
sudo iptables -A INPUT -p tcp -s 0/0 -d $SERVER_IP \
  --sport 513:65535 \
  --dport 8080 -m state \
  --state NEW,ESTABLISHED -j ACCEPT
# In the next line replace 3022 with your choice for the SSH port
sudo iptables -A OUTPUT -p tcp -s $SERVER_IP -d 0/0 \
  --sport 3022 \
  --dport 513:65535 -m state \
  --state NEW,ESTABLISHED -j ACCEPT
sudo iptables -A OUTPUT -p tcp -s $SERVER_IP -d 0/0 \
  --sport 8080 \
  --dport 513:65535 -m state \
  --state NEW,ESTABLISHED -j ACCEPT
sudo iptables -A INPUT -j DROP
sudo iptables -A OUTPUT -j DROP
```

The rules are effective right away, but I bet you don't want to do that again. And since you want them active at every boot, too, there are a couple more actions.

Save your *firewall* configuration.

```
youruser@yourhost:~$ sudo sh -c "/sbin/iptables-save > /etc/firewall.conf"
```

With the configuration in a known location, we can write a *small init script, /etc/init.d/ iptables*, that saves the configuration when the server stops and loads the configuration when the server starts.

Most Linux distributions have an init script for iptables. Ubuntu does not.

```
#!/bin/bash
# chkconfig: 2345 08 92
# description:  saves and loads iptables firewall
# config: /etc/firewall.conf

start() {
  /sbin/iptables-restore < /etc/firewall.conf
}

stop() {
  /sbin/iptables-save > /etc/firewall.conf
}

case "$1" in
  start)
    start
    ;;
  stop)
    stop
    ;;
  restart)
    stop
    sleep 3
    start
    ;;
  *)
    echo "Usage: $0 {start|stop}"
    exit 1
esac

exit $?
```

Activate the *init script*.

```
youruser@yourhost:~$ sudo update-rc.d iptables defaults 08 92
update-rc.d: warning: /etc/init.d/iptables missing LSB information
update-rc.d: see <http://wiki.debian.org/LSBInitScripts>
 Adding system startup for /etc/init.d/iptables ...
   /etc/rc0.d/K92iptables -> ../init.d/iptables
   /etc/rc1.d/K92iptables -> ../init.d/iptables
   /etc/rc6.d/K92iptables -> ../init.d/iptables
   /etc/rc2.d/S08iptables -> ../init.d/iptables
   /etc/rc3.d/S08iptables -> ../init.d/iptables
   /etc/rc4.d/S08iptables -> ../init.d/iptables
   /etc/rc5.d/S08iptables -> ../init.d/iptables
```

Tunneling

We are going to connect the 1060 port on our local (client) system to the 1060 port on the remote (server) system. In order not to get false results, make sure you do not have a NetKernel instance running on your local system.

The command to set up the tunnel is the same on a Linux client and on a Windows client (under Cygwin).

```
$ ssh -L 1060:yourserver:1060 youruser@yourserver -p 3022
youruser@yourserver's password:
Linux yourserver 2.6.32-36-generic #79-Ubuntu SMP Tue Nov 8 22:29:53 UTC 2011 x86_64
GNU/Linux
Ubuntu 10.04.3 LTS

Welcome to Ubuntu!
 * Documentation:  https://help.ubuntu.com/

youruser@yourhost:~$
```

As long as the above connection is open, you can reach the remote Backend HTTPFulcrum at *http://localhost:1060* on your local server.

Source Version Control

You need it. You know you do!

Raison d'être[1]

This section is going to be a bit of a rant. You've been warned!

Statements

- *Backups* protect you against faulty hardware.
- *Source Version Control* protects you against faulty developers.

Discussion

Most people will endorse these two statements. We all know why the Challenger (*http://en.wikipedia.org/wiki/Space_Shuttle_Challenger_disaster*) crashed, and we all know that the *I* in *RAID* (*http://en.wikipedia.org/wiki/RAID*) stands for *Inexpensive*.[2] And you might not believe this, but take the word of an ex-storage manager (me), the disks in your home PC are exactly the same ones that you can find in those very expensive storage arrays from EMC^2, Hitachi, HP, IBM, and so on, exactly the same (even interchangeable if you replace the casing). Did you ever wonder why those arrays have up to 10 spare disks inside and why your company had to install a revolving door (and issue an access-at-all-times badge) for the storage technician replacing faulty disks?

And yet, how many of you have a decent (regular, incremental) backup of your home PC? It does, in this digital era, contain all photographs of your loved ones, your tax forms, your bank statements, and so on. Are those not important, then?

---

1. Reason of existence.

2. Or *Independent*.

And yet, we all know that the better class of developer sometimes likes to ride his/her horse tangent off into some unknown direction. This is allowed (and often encouraged in the more successful companies, because although nine-tenths of it will be a useless exercise, the one-tenth pays the whole company for a year), but is it not important to be able to quickly revert back to the last working code?

Conclusion

Backups and source version control are necessary. Some people say it's a choice between safety and paranoia. The Challenger crew would no doubt love to hear their explanation.

 In the first version of this appendix, there was a rather pedantic[3] and hopelessly technical setup of a manual version control system for your modules. In a second iteration, I actually developed a source version control module. While it worked, it didn't *work* within the book.

What follows is the approach close to what the *1060 Research* team uses. We'll set up Eclipse to develop a second version of *First Module* and use a Subversion plugin and a local Subversion repository to get the job done.

 The choice for Subversion is not random. The Subversion setup fits NetKernel's modular setup like a glove. If you are interested in the full background story, check it at *http://wiki.netkernel.org/wink/wiki/Net Kernel/News/1/47/September_24th_2010#Modular_Source_Control*.

Setup

Before I start, let me repeat that whatever editor feels good for you (and makes you productive) is fine by me. However, in a book on the basics, an appendix that describes a (not "the") development environment does have its place. And you know, even you, oh mighty wizard of Notepad (substitute with your favorite editor), may learn something from this appendix. I know I did by writing it.

Eclipse

Download *Eclipse* for your OS. If you are confused by the different choices, *Eclipse Classic* will do just fine. I'll assume you made that choice for the remainder of this appendix.

---

3. Know thyself.

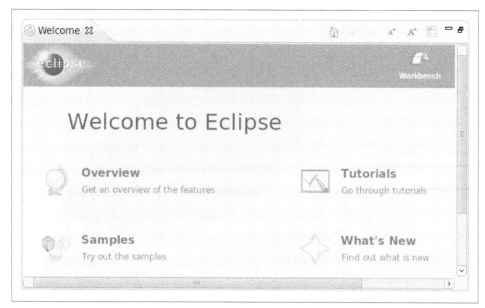

Figure E-1. Welcome tab

 Especially on Linux systems, you can install Eclipse (and most of its extra tools and plugins) from the package management tool running on the system. I personally think this is a bad idea. For one thing, you are only going to need Eclipse on a development system. Secondly, Eclipse is all about the extra tools and plugins and which ones you use and which ones you don't. So, if your work environment dictates a stable uniform environment, packages are a valid choice (but remember, once you use packages, you shouldn't do updates or plugin installs through Eclipse itself!). Otherwise, install it yourself.

Install *Eclipse* by unpacking the archive you downloaded in the location where you want it. It will produce an *eclipse* directory there.

Start *Eclipse* by running the executable in the *Eclipse* directory. You'll be asked for a workspace location, and enter *one*. After Eclipse has loaded you should get a Welcome tab (Figure E-1).

Close the *Welcome tab*, and you get the base view to work with (Figure E-2).

Subversion Repository

I am going to assume you have Subversion installed on the system where you are going to do the development, either under Cygwin on Windows (see Appendix B for instructions) or natively on a Linux system (if not, your package manager tool will contain it). Verify *this*.

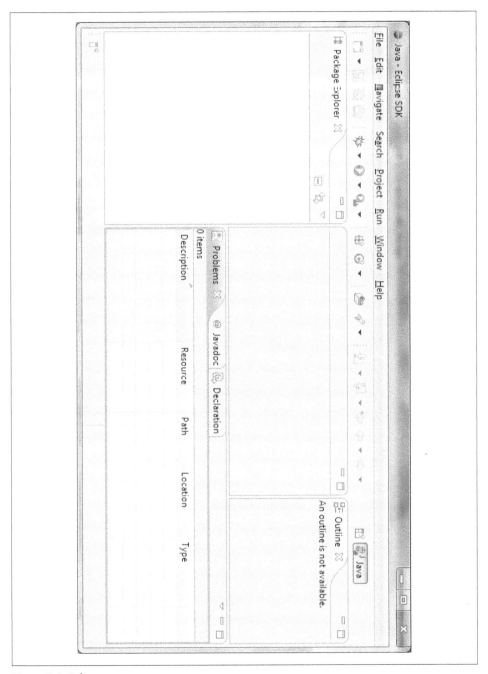

Figure E-2. Eclipse

```
svn --version --quiet
```

Create a new *Subversion repository* as follows :

```
svnadmin create /cygdrive/c/svneclipse_book
```

 Your chosen directory may, of course, differ. On a Linux system, you may want to prepend *sudo* to the command if you're creating the directory in a location you don't have permissions for.

Customize Eclipse

No installation is complete without some customization. Eclipse is no exception.

Extra tools

The *Install New Software* option is neatly hidden in the *Help* menu of Eclipse. Select it.

In order to get an overview of all installable tools/plugins/softwares, select *--All Available Sites--* in the *Work with* field. Be patient as the result may take a while to load.

I want you to select and install the following *tools* that you can find under the *Web, XML, Java EE, and OSGi Enterprise Development* heading :

```
Eclipse Web Developer Tools
Eclipse XML Editors and Tools
Eclipse XSL Developer Tools
```

Along the way, you'll have to accept the *Eclipse Public License*, and at the end, Eclipse will restart.

These tools—but you already deduced that from their names—make XML-based development in Eclipse a lot easier (Figure E-3).

NetKernel specific

By changing a couple of preferences, we can make an Eclipse project fit like a glove to a NetKernel module. You can find the *Preferences* option in the *Window* menu. Select it.

The first thing we are going to change is the *Source and output folder* setting that you can find under *Java - Build Path*. Change the setting to *Project*, and select *Apply* (Figure E-4).

Underneath *Build Path*, you can also find *User Libraries*. Select that *option*. If you've just started, you'll probably get an empty window. Select *New user library* (Figure E-5).

Enter *NetKernel* in the *User Library Name* field, and select *OK*.

Next (with the NetKernel user library selected), select *Add JARs*. You need to add the following jar files:

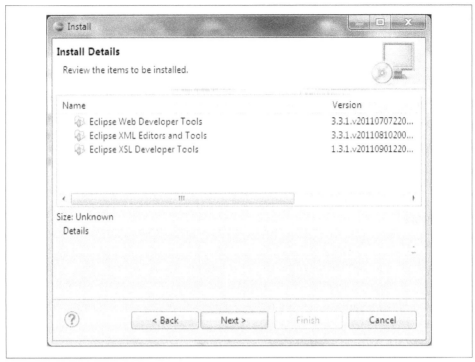

Figure E-3. Eclipse XML tools

```
urn.com.ten60.core.layer0-x.x.x.jar
urn.com.ten60.module.standard-x.x.x.jar
urn.com.ten60.core.netkernel.api-x.x.x.jar
urn.com.ten60.core.netkernel.impl-x.x.x.jar
```

You can probably guess where those come from. That's right, from *[install]/lib* (with [install] being the directory where you installed NetKernel).

When all jars are added (Figure E-6), <u>select</u> OK to keep your *Preferences* changes.

You are now ready to start a new project.

New Eclipse Project

Everything has been set up so that one Eclipse Project coincides with one NetKernel module. Are you ready?

Creation

<u>Select</u> *New - Java Project* from the *File* menu.

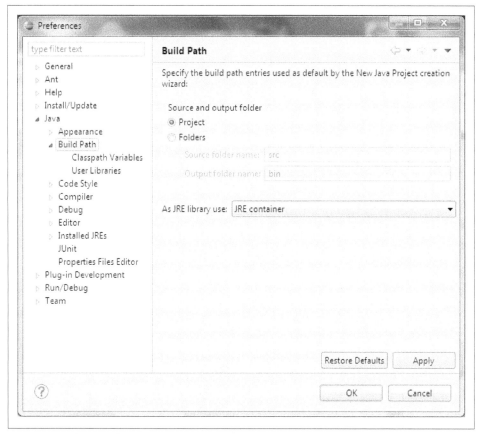

Figure E-4. Eclipse preferences

 Yes, I am aware of the fact that *First Module* does not contain one iota of Java. Most core NetKernel modules do, however, and we are following the same structure.

On the first screen of the dialog (Figure E-7) you are presented with, you only have to enter the project/module name (without a version number).

```
urn.org.netkernelbook.chapter2.firstmodule
```

<u>Select</u> *Next*.

On the second screen of the dialog, you have to add the user library we created earlier :

1. <u>Select</u> the *Library* tab.
2. <u>Select</u> *Add Library*.
3. <u>Select</u> library type *User Library*, and <u>select</u> *Next*.

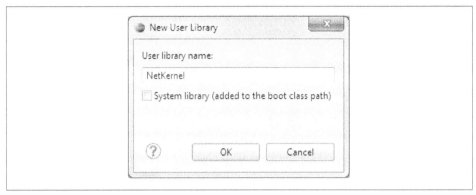

Figure E-5. New user library

4. Select *NetKernel* and select *Finish*.

Now, you select *Finish* for the dialog (Figure E-8) itself, and the project will be created.

Sources

It is a good exercise to (re)create *First Module* from scratch now. Seriously. While you might make mistakes (again), that is the only way to learn.

So, select the *project* in the *Package Explorer*, and create the necessary files and folders through the options *New - File* and *New - Folder* in the context menu (Figure E-9).

There are two things worth mentioning here. Since it is a Java project, Eclipse automatically shows folders as packages. I did not create a folder *etc.system*, I created a folder *etc* and a folder *system* underneath that. What Eclipse shows makes no difference to the end result. It can look confusing if you are not aware of it, though.

Secondly, Eclipse does not know about *dpml* and *groovy* files. So I added those in the *Preferences* under *General - Editors - File Associations* and linked them to the (Eclipse) XML Editor and the (Eclipse) Java Editor, respectively. It is not a problem if you don't do this, but otherwise, it might be your default editor that fires up (instead of the inline Eclipse editor) when you select them.

As soon as you've got a couple of folders and files, you are ready for the next step.

Source Version Control

Our Eclipse installation comes with the tools for *Source Version Control*. Select the *project* in the *Package Explorer* and you'll find a *Team* submenu in the context menu. Sadly enough, by default only CVS is supported.

What we need is an Eclipse plugin/tool that works with Subversion. Several exist; I've selected Subclipse for this appendix.

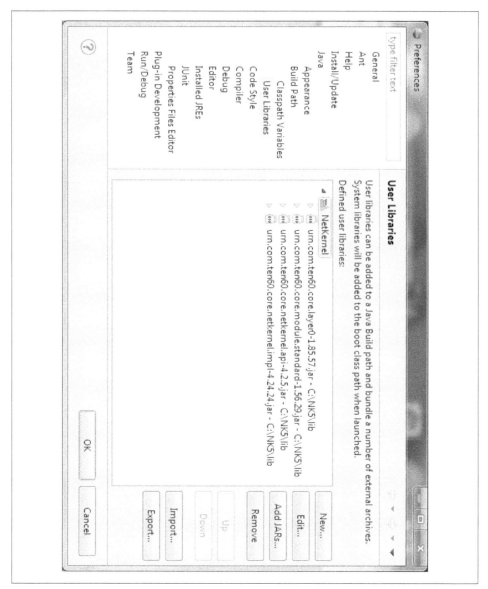

Figure E-6. NetKernel user library

You don't need to download anything from there because installing and updating is done from Eclipse itself. Subclipse is, however, not listed in the softwares available from the default repositories (or sites), so what you need is the site where Subclipse resides. Since this can change quickly, here's how to find it :

1. <u>Browse</u> to *the Subclipse site (http://subclipse.tigris.org/)*.

Figure E-7. New Java project

2. Select the *Download and Install* tab.

3. Obviously, you have to check whether your version of Eclipse is supported in the current Subclipse release, but let us assume it is. Then you can find what you need labeled *Eclipse update site URL*.

With the above information, you can go to—yes, indeed—the *Install New Software* option of the *Help* menu. Enter the *site URL* in the *Work with* field, and enter. You should now see Subclipse appear in the list.

Select and install only the *required parts* of Subclipse (Figure E-10).

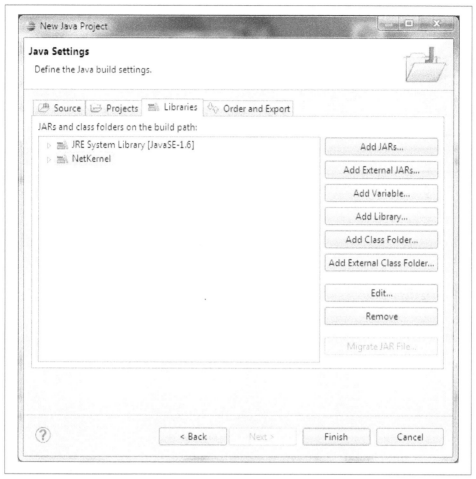

Figure E-8. Project settings

Use the same procedure as earlier in this appendix, but you will get a warning about *unsigned content* (Figure E-11). You may safely continue.

Before we start using Subclipse, I want you to change a convenience setting in the *Preferences*. Select *Team*, and set the *Perspective* option to *None*. It is just a personal preference that I use to keep an easy overview of everything.

With Subclipse installed, select the *project* in the *Package Explorer*, and then *select* the *Share Project* option in the *Team* submenu of the context menu.

You now have the choice (see Figure E-12) between CVS and SVN (SubVersioN). Select the *latter* and then *Next*.

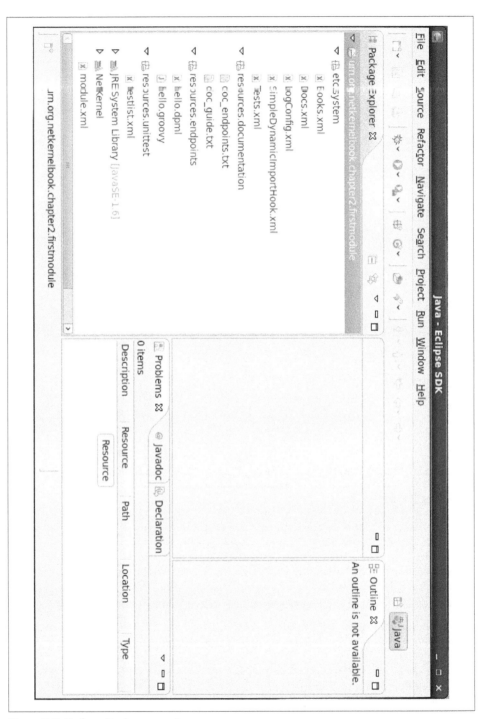

Figure E-9. Package Explorer overview

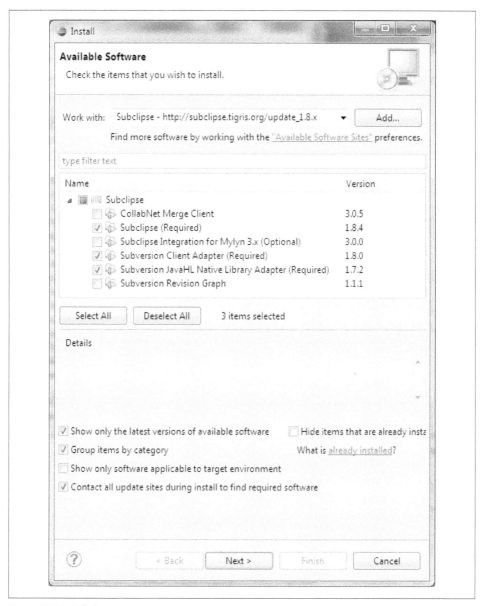

Figure E-10. Subclipse

Eclipse asks us for the (Subversion) repository location. We defined a local Subversion repository earlier: this is where you have to remember where you defined it. Since it is local, you can use the *file:* protocol. Enter the *url* and then *Next* (Figure E-13).

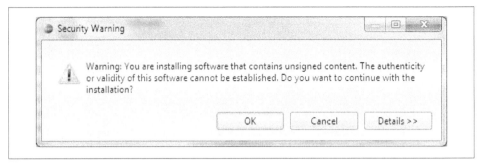

Figure E-11. Install warning

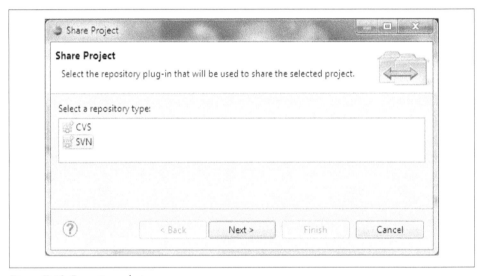

Figure E-12. Repository choice

I used a local repository with the *file:* protocol to keep things simple. The above procedure works just as well with a Subversion repository somewhere on the Internet. The URL might then look like this:

```
http://x.unfuddle.com/svn/x_modules/
```

By the way, do not try that URL. The *x* is supposed to be replaced with your repository name on said provider's site.

Eclipse now asks you what folder name you want to use. The project name is fine, so just select *Next* (Figure E-14).

Read what the *final dialog* has to say. The first time I did this, I was surprised a bit later that it didn't commit my files to the repository. It doesn't; it prepares the folder in the repository (Figure E-15).

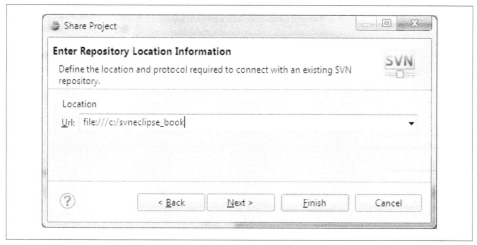

Figure E-13. Repository location

Figure E-14. Repository folder name

When you are ready, <u>select</u> *Finish*. If you are asked to open a new perspective, <u>an-swer</u> *No* (Figure E-16).

In the *Package Explorer*, you'll notice that the project is marked with an *asterisk*.[4] Whenever this is the case, there is a discrepancy between your sources and the Subversion repository.

---

4. Is it so strange to confuse this character with this *character* (*http://en.wikipedia.org/wiki/Asterix _(character)*)?

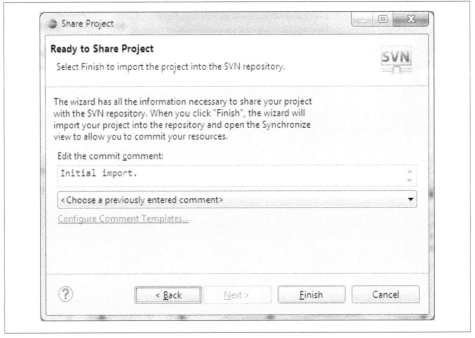

Figure E-15. Initial import

That in itself is not a problem (adding one blank in any source file will cause it), but you should know why there is a discrepancy. Currently, the issue is that we have not committed the sources to the repository yet.

Select the *project* in the *Package Explorer*, and then select the *Commit* option in the *Team* submenu of the context menu (Figure E-17).

Enter a *comment* for the commit, and then select *OK*.

Figure E-18 shows how your *Package Explorer* should look before and after every development session, with everything cleanly commited, sources and Subversion repository in sync.

I could go on with best practices in regard to *Source Version Control* for another book. For Subversion, it has already been written (*http://svnbook.red-bean.com/*), and not by me, I might add.

Deployment

Only one mystery remains, and that is deployment. How does one deploy from Eclipse to the running NetKernel instance?

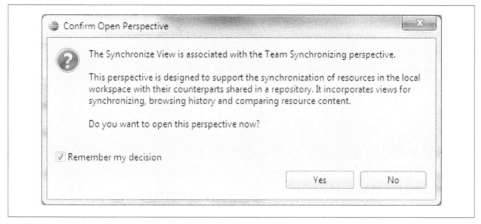

Figure E-16. New perspective

The magic word is *export*. <u>Select</u> the *project* in the *Package Explorer*, and then <u>select</u> *Export*.

As you'll see, there are lots of possibilities for an export. <u>Select</u> *General - File System* and then *Next* (Figure E-19).

Before you enter the export location, you've got to deselect a couple of things first:

```
file        .classpath
file        .project
directory   .settings
```

All of these are in the project root directory. Strictly speaking you do not need to deselect them. I just like my deployments to be clean. Eclipse meta-information does not belong in there (Figure E-20).

The *To directory* is obviously the module's full path-with-version in the *project-modules* directory.

<u>Select</u> *Finish*, and magic happens. If this is the first time you export the project to the given directory, you have to confirm the creation (Figure E-21).

All that remains for you to do is add (or change, if you deployed a new version) the entry in *[install]/etc/modules.xml*.

 Once the Subversion repository is linked to the project sources, it is linked, and you have to actively break the link if you no longer require a repository. The export options, on the contrary, are not project specific. So, take good care if you work with several projects at the same time. You wouldn't be the first (I was there before you) to deploy project X to the directory of project Y.

Figure E-17. Initial commit

On Linux, the deployment will be owned by the user running Eclipse. Make sure this user can deploy to the *project-modules* directory, and also make sure the user running NetKernel can access the deployment. To make things easy, you could use the same user for both tasks. On a single developer development machine, this is definitely the preferred method, but otherwise you'll have to do some group magic.

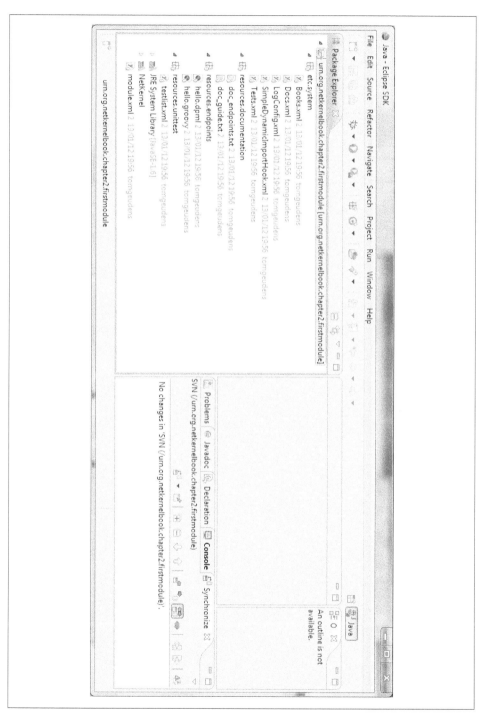

Figure E-18. Package Explorer overview

Figure E-19. Export destination

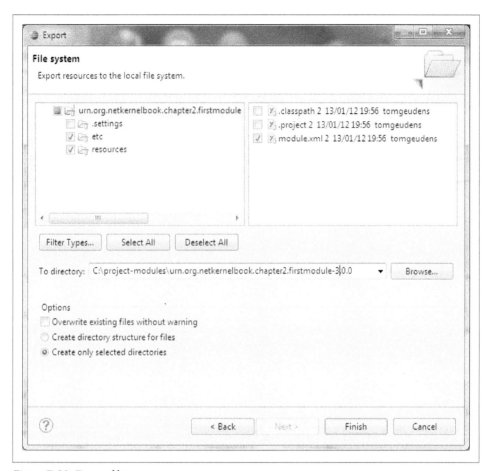

Figure E-20. Export filesystem

Figure E-21. Create export directory

Examples and Solutions

Example—Limiter

A *Limiter* endpoint takes care of unwanted side effects in a space.[1]

Setup

Consider the following rootspace definition:

```
<rootspace
  name="Limiter Demo - Services"
  public="true"
  uri="urn:org:netkernelbook:chapter2:limiter:services">
  <fileset>
    <regex>res:/etc/system/SimpleDynamicImportHook.xml</regex>
  </fileset>

  <fileset>
    <regex>res:/limiterdemo/(.*)</regex>
    <rewrite>res:/resources/$1</rewrite>
  </fileset>
</rootspace>
```

The functionality of this rootspace could be described as *providing access to anything in the resources directory*.

With the following content for *SimpleDynamicImportHook.xml*, that means you provide access to anything in the resources directory to the *whole wide world*.[2]

```
<connection>
  <type>HTTPFulcrum</type>
</connection>
```

---

1. Pretty much like Jupiter or, more dramatically, a black hole.

2. If your server is connected to the Internet, of course.

Let us also create a couple of things in the resources directory. First, there's a file *limiter_demo_allowed.txt*:

```
http://periodicvideos.com/
http://www.sixtysymbols.com/
```

There's also a file *limiter_demo_not_allowed.xml*.

```
<general>
  <password>ThisIsThePasswordIUseEverywhere</password>
</general>
```

The issue

http://localhost:8080/limiterdemo/limiter_demo_not_allowed.xml

The solution

```
<rootspace
  name="Limiter Demo - Services"
  public="true"
  uri="urn:org:netkernelbook:chapter2:limiter:services">
  <fileset>
    <regex>res:/etc/system/SimpleDynamicImportHook.xml</regex>
  </fileset>

  <fileset>
    <regex>res:/limiterdemo/(.*)</regex>
    <rewrite>res:/resources/$1</rewrite>
  </fileset>

  <endpoint>
    <prototype>Limiter</prototype>
    <grammar>res:/limiterdemo/
      <regex>.*\.xml</regex>
    </grammar>
  </endpoint>

  <import>
    <uri>urn:org:netkernel:ext:layer1</uri>
    <private/>
  </import>
</rootspace>
```

It speaks for itself, does it not? The Limiter endpoint is provided by Layer1, and the prototype definition expects a grammar to filter other endpoints.

Verification

http://localhost:8080/limiterdemo/limiter_demo_not_allowed.xml (Figure F-1).

Hold on, we went wrong somewhere . . .

Figure F-1. Limiter verification

The Correct Solution

```
<rootspace
  name="Limiter Demo - Services"
  public="true"
  uri="urn:org:netkernelbook:chapter2:limiter:services">
  <fileset>
    <regex>res:/etc/system/SimpleDynamicImportHook.xml</regex>
  </fileset>

  <endpoint>
    <prototype>Limiter</prototype>
    <grammar>res:/limiterdemo/
      <regex>.*\.xml</regex>
    </grammar>
  </endpoint>

  <fileset>
    <regex>res:/limiterdemo/(.*)</regex>
    <rewrite>res:/resources/$1</rewrite>
  </fileset>

  <import>
    <uri>urn:org:netkernel:ext:layer1</uri>
    <private/>
  </import>
</rootspace>
```

Within a space resolution, is *top to bottom*. If a request finds a matching endpoint, all that follows is being ignored. So, we have to make sure the potentially embarrassing requests are *limited* before they find another match.

Another verification

http://localhost:8080/limiterdemo/limiter_demo_not_allowed.xml (Figure F-2)

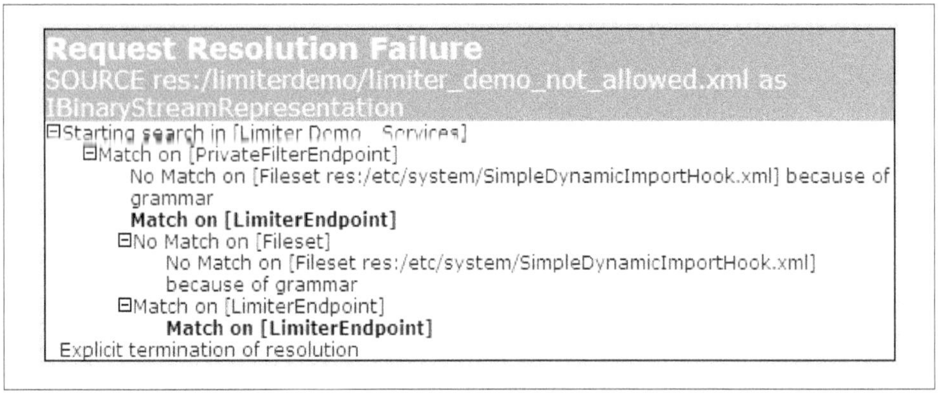

```
Request Resolution Failure
SOURCE res:/limiterdemo/limiter_demo_not_allowed.xml as
IBinaryStreamRepresentation
⊟Starting search in [Limiter Demo - Services]
    ⊟Match on [PrivateFilterEndpoint]
        No Match on [Fileset res:/etc/system/SimpleDynamicImportHook.xml] because of
        grammar
        Match on [LimiterEndpoint]
    ⊟No Match on [Fileset]
        No Match on [Fileset res:/etc/system/SimpleDynamicImportHook.xml]
        because of grammar
    ⊟Match on [LimiterEndpoint]
        Match on [LimiterEndpoint]
Explicit termination of resolution
```

Figure F-2. Limiter verification

Conclusion

I'm aware that the example is contrived and that the issue could have been resolved in a number of ways (starting with a better regular expression on the fileset definition). The fact remains that the *Limiter* is an efficient constraint tool, allowing for pragmatism and simplicity.

Solution—Error in third test ExtJS Server module

The third test of the ExtJS Server module (the one on version 3.3.1) fails with an *assertionException*.

How you can troubleshoot requests is discussed elsewhere, but the problem in this case is that there's a special character in the *res:/ExtJS-3.3.1/doc/index.html* that is perfectly valid as HTML, but not when we process it in our xpath evaluation. Open that *index.html* file in a text editor, and replace … with …. All should now be well.

Solution—xrl:resolve

In Chapter 7, you had to figure out why a link generated with *xrl:resolve* did not work.

Well, if you select the link, the URL in your browser is *http://localhost:1060/chapter7/ testfile.txt*. Now, ask yourself the question: is our chapter 7 module exposed to the Backend HTTPFulcrum?

In the module itself? No.

In the introspect module where we imported it? No.

The *Scripting Playpen* itself is, but we used <private/> in the import, which is good practice! If you want the link to work, remove <private/> from the import of the chapter

7 module. Put it back after you're satisfied, though if we wanted that module exposed to the Backend HTTPFulcrum permanently, we'd do it in the module itself.

About the Author

At the age of 15, Tom Geudens's parents gave him a choice: either become a baker or go into IT. That Christmas, after Santa brought an MSX home computer, the choice was made. At twenty, and with a bachelor's in IT under his belt, he joined the IT department of Colruyt, a Belgian retailer that specialized in 'Lowest Price' and doing this through automation. Recently, Tom set up his own IT consultancy company, Elephant Bird Consulting. He has worked with technologies from PL/1 through HPUX and Linux, and battled distributed applications development and configuration management issues.

Have it your way.

Get even more for your money.

Join the O'Reilly Community, and register the O'Reilly books you own. It's free, and you'll get:

- $4.99 ebook upgrade offer
- 40% upgrade offer on O'Reilly print books
- Membership discounts on books and events
- Free lifetime updates to ebooks and videos
- Multiple ebook formats, DRM FREE
- Participation in the O'Reilly community
- Newsletters
- Account management
- 100% Satisfaction Guarantee

Signing up is easy:

1. **Go to: oreilly.com/go/register**
2. **Create an O'Reilly login.**
3. **Provide your address.**
4. **Register your books.**

Note: English-language books only

To order books online:
oreilly.com/store

For questions about products or an order:
orders@oreilly.com

To sign up to get topic-specific email announcements and/or news about upcoming books, conferences, special offers, and new technologies:
elists@oreilly.com

For technical questions about book content:
booktech@oreilly.com

To submit new book proposals to our editors:
proposals@oreilly.com

O'Reilly books are available in multiple DRM-free ebook formats. For more information:
oreilly.com/ebooks

O'REILLY®

Spreading the knowledge of innovators　　　　　　　　oreilly.com

©2010 O'Reilly Media, Inc. O'Reilly logo is a registered trademark of O'Reilly Media, Inc. 00000

9 781449 322526